That Patchwork Place®

Traditional Blocks
Meet Appliqué

Deborah J. Moffett-Hall

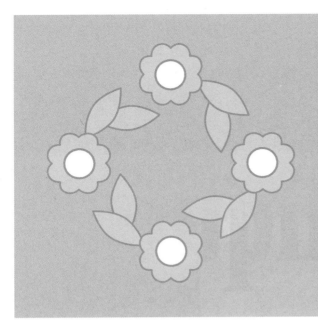

Dedication

This book is dedicated with love and thanks to my family and friends who helped make it possible:

My husband, Scott, who listened to quilt talk for months, made helpful suggestions, and offered constant encouragement.

Our daughter, Michelle, who is always interested in my projects and understands when Mom "has to work."

And my mother, Jane Moffett, who said, "I knew you could do it."

Credits

Technical Editor .... Ursula Reikes
Editorial Director .... Kerry I. Hoffman
Managing Editor .... Greg Sharp
Design Director .... Judy Petry
Text and Cover Designer .... Cheryl Stevenson
Production Assistants .... Dani Ritchardson
　　　　　　　　　　　　　　　　　　　　　　　　Claudia L'Heureux
Copy Editor .... Tina Cook
Proofreader .... Melissa Riesland
Illustrators .... Laurel Strand
　　　　　　　　　　　　　　　　　　　　　　　Lisa McKenney
Photographer .... Brent Kane

Traditional Blocks Meet Appliqué
© 1996 by Deborah J. Moffett-Hall
That Patchwork Place, Inc., PO Box 118
Bothell, WA 98041-0118 USA

Printed in the United States of America
01 00 99 98 97 96   6 5 4 3 2 1

Library of Congress Cataloging-in-Publication Data

Moffett-Hall, Deborah J.
　　Traditional blocks meet appliqué / Deborah J. Moffett-Hall.
　　　　p. cm.
　　ISBN 1-56477-123-7
　　1. Patchwork—Patterns. 2. Appliqué—Patterns.
　3. Quilting—Patterns. I. Title
　TT835.M645   1996
　746.46—dc20　　　　　　　　　　　　　　　　95-50550
　　　　　　　　　　　　　　　　　　　　　　　　　　　　CIP

MISSION STATEMENT

We are dedicated to providing quality products and services that inspire creativity. We work together to enrich the lives we touch.

That Patchwork Place is a financially responsible ESOP company.

Acknowledgments

To Beth Hertz, and Marla and Bob Moyer, thanks for your helpful comments and terrific sewing skills.

To the Electric Quilt Company, for a wonderful computer program that makes designing projects on my PC a joy.

And to Noltings Long Arm Quilting Machine manufacturers, for a quality product that enabled me to quilt all the projects in this book without a hitch or a hiccup.

Contents

INTRODUCTION

FABRIC

When a person creates something unique, be it built, painted, written, or quilted, one of the first questions asked by others is: Where do you get your ideas? Many ideas start with the basics, and in quilting this means the traditional patterns we have come to know and love.

The quilt patterns in this book started with a question I often ask myself when brainstorming: What if? What if I put appliqué designs in the open areas of the Double Irish Chain pattern? What if I combine other traditional patterns with the appliqué blocks?

My favorite designing trick is to combine traditional and new blocks in such a way that the original outline of the block or blocks is blurred by the emergence of an exciting secondary pattern. I then like to add an appliqué design in the spaces created by the interplay of blocks. Sometimes the traditional block pattern and the newly created interplay pattern take turns coming forward. These dynamic quilts can look very different from one moment to the next.

Using the same basic appliqué block—a plain block with four cornerstones—I played with various traditional patterns on my computer and selected my favorites for this book. I changed some of the traditional blocks slightly to improve the secondary pattern lines, but the basic feel of the block remains true. The resulting quilts have their roots in tradition, but it's tradition with a bit of spice, an element of surprise.

The appliqué blocks are the same size in each of the quilts, so you can mix and match the appliqué designs with any of the traditional blocks in the book. The pieced traditional blocks range in difficulty from quick and easy to moderately time consuming, but strip-piecing and rotary-cutting methods speed things along nicely. The appliqué designs also range from easy, simple shapes to more intricate patterns and can be stitched by hand or machine. A how-to section on machine appliqué is included to get you started on an heirloom that will be a grand new twist on tradition.

Selecting Fabrics for Your Quilts

Good quality, 100% cotton fabric is an excellent choice for most quilting projects. By good quality, I mean a tightly woven fabric that doesn't show distinct space between the fibers when you hold it up to a light source. The exception is homespun or woven plaids, which are coarsely woven on purpose.

Beware of a stiff piece of fabric. It may be an inferior weave that has been ultrasaturated with dye to give it more body and fill in the loose weave. The excess dye will wash out, leaving you with cheesecloth.

Good quality cotton is consistent in weight before and after washing. However, prewashing does remove the sizing, which may affect the feel of the fabric.

Cotton fabrics cut cleanly and fray less than other fabrics. Cotton is also easier to sew because the layers tend to grip each other as they go through the machine. Pressing is easier as well. You can even finger-press small seams.

Specialty fabrics, such as metallics and silks, can be used for special effects with stunning results, but the finished quilt will require greater care when it comes to washing and storage. Be sure to check the bolt end for recommended fabric care. Some cotton- and polyester-blend fabrics tend to pill with use and washing, but they are fine for a wall hanging that will not see much of either.

Yardage requirements in this book are based on 42" of usable fabric width to allow for any shrinkage or manufacturing variances.

Coordinating Prints and Solids

When I walk into my favorite quilt shop to purchase fabric for my next project, I have three things with me:

* A sketch of the design with the various pattern pieces colored in light, medium, and dark values, and the yardage required for each;
* An uncolored copy of the pattern in case I change my mind; and
* A pencil to make notes.

The first fabric I look for is the primary print. A primary print is one that determines the tone and colors of all the other fabrics in the quilt. It may not be a major element in the finished quilt, but it is the starting point for coordinating your fabric selections.

Find a primary print that you love, one in which the colors sing to you and the pattern charms you. Now take it to a window and look at it in natural light. Are the colors still singing? The indoor lighting in most stores can greatly alter fabric colors. Fluorescent lights cast a green tint and incandescent lights can be blue, yellow, or pink in hue, all of which can mask the true colors of your chosen fabric. If your primary print is just as perfect in daylight, proceed to the next step.

Examine the overall look of your primary print. Using the colored sketch of your pattern as a guide, determine where to use the primary print in your pattern. Keep in mind the scale or size of the print when deciding where to place it in your block. Small- to medium-scale prints work well in most any size pattern piece. Large-scale prints, however, need a larger area to show them off to their best advantage.

Do not use busy, large-scale prints for the background of the appliqué blocks; the appliqué pieces will be lost in the pattern. Solids and small-scale or tone-on-tone prints work best for backgrounds. If your pattern does not have a place for your large-scale print, consider using it for the border.

Next, select colors from your primary print and assign each a place in your pattern. Remember that dark colors make a stronger statement than light colors. A 2" dark square equals a 4" light square in the overall balance of your quilt.

Now carry the primary print with you as you walk through the store, and pull out any bolts that match the colors you have selected. Try to find at least two fabrics in each color family, and select solids and small-scale and medium prints from which to make your final choices. Stack the bolts by color family and unwrap enough of your primary print to drape across one side of the stacked bolts. Step back and squint (or take off your glasses). Does one fabric jump out from the rest? Discard it, or use it for very small accents in the quilt.

Take each bolt and your primary print to the window to make sure the colors are true. Discard any that do not pass the window test and select another from that color family and try again. If you have two fabrics of a given color family, say pink, that both pass the window test, then look at the scale or pattern of the other fabrics you have already approved. Select the pink that is different in scale or pattern from the others. You want a mix of solids, tone-on-tones, small prints, and medium prints to give your quilt visual texture.

NOTE

Try to use the same white, off-white, or ecru in any one project. If you start with off-white as one of your colors or the background of your print, then the other prints, if they have any white areas, should also be off-white rather than bright white or ecru.

Preparing the Fabric

I confess, most of the time I do not prewash my fabrics. Fabric has more body while the sizing is in it, and I like the way it handles. The corners of my triangles don't droop while I'm trying to match them, nor do they dive down into the feed dogs as I sew.

I do buy top quality fabric, and I do keep a wary eye on reds since red is the worst culprit in the bleeding department. I test fabrics by sewing a small swatch of the dark color in question to a scrap of white. Then I wet them both with tepid water and watch for the colors to bleed. If they bleed, I wash them. If they do not, I submit the samples to the pressing test. Move a hot iron from the dark color toward the white fabric a couple times. If the heat transfers the color, prewash. Be sure to clean your iron after this test.

If you want to be safe, prewash all your fabrics using a mild detergent, and tumble or line dry until barely damp. Fold the fabric in half, matching selvages, and press. If you prefer, use spray sizing while you press to restore some of the body to the fabric.

Gathering Supplies

Sewing Machine: For machine appliqué, you need a machine that has a zigzag capability. A walking foot or darning foot is essential for machine quilting.

Thread: Use good quality cotton or cotton-wrapped polyester thread.

Needles: Use the size indicated in your machine handbook or size 70/10 or 80/12.

Pins: Long, thin quilters' pins, with easy-to-see round heads, are great for both piecing and holding appliqués for machine stitching.

Template Plastic: There are many types of clear or frosted plastics available for making templates. I like the frosted type and use a fine-point permanent marker to trace the shape and any grain lines or instructions directly onto the template. The permanent marker does not rub off onto the fabric during use.

Marking Tools: Any of the fabric marking tools available will do the job. Just be sure to test them on fabric to make sure you can see the lines and remove the marks easily.

Rotary-Cutting Tools: You need a rotary cutter with a good blade (no nicks), a cutting mat to protect your blade and work surface, and clear acrylic rulers, including a 6" x 24" ruler and a 12½" square. The Bias Square® ruler is great for cutting bias squares (presewn squares consisting of half-square triangles.)

Rotary Cutting

All cutting measurements include ¼"-wide seam allowances unless otherwise noted.

NOTE

The following directions are for right-handed people. If you are left-handed, either reverse everything or walk around to the other side of the table to make your cuts.

1. Align the selvages and the grain lines as best you can. Sometimes tugging at opposite corners helps straighten out-of-kilter yardage.

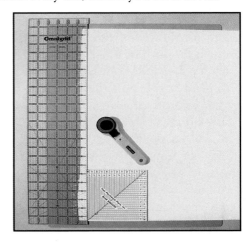

2. Place the widest portion of the cutting mat on your table vertically to accommodate the width of the folded fabric. (If your cutting mat is less than 23" wide, fold the fabric again, carefully aligning the selvages with the folded edge.)

3. Place the fabric on the mat with the folded edge closest to you and the cut edge to your left. Spread the rest of the fabric to your right.

4. To square up the edge of the fabric, place either a square ruler or a sheet of paper on the folded edge of the fabric and line up the long edge of a 24"-long ruler with the left edge of your guide. Slide both items left or right as needed until the long ruler just covers the entire ragged edge. Remove the square ruler or piece of paper. Holding the long ruler firmly in place with your left hand, make a smooth cut along the right-hand edge of the ruler. Always cut away from your body. Remember, that blade is sharp! Also, get in the habit of closing your blade after every cut, before you set it down.

5. Align the required measurement on the long ruler with the newly cut edge of the fabric. Holding the ruler firmly with your left hand, cut with a smooth steady stroke *away* from your body.

You may have to resquare the left edge as you shift additional fabric onto the mat. As a rule of thumb, it's a good idea to check the square of the edge after every 3 to 4 cuts.

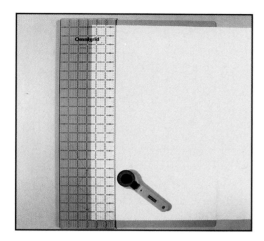

A. To cut squares, cut strips the required width, then turn the strip on your cutting board and remove the selvages. Align the required measurement for the square on the left-hand edge and cut as many squares as needed.

B. To make half-square triangles, cut a square ⅞" larger than the finished short side of the required triangle to allow for seam allowances. Cut the square once diagonally. The short sides of the half-square triangles are on the straight grain of the fabric.

C. To make quarter-square triangles, cut a square 1¼" larger than the finished long side of the required triangle to allow for seam allowances. Cut the square twice diagonally. The long side of the quarter-square triangle is on the straight grain of the fabric.

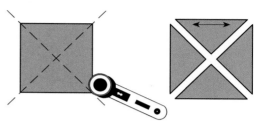

D. Use easy strip-piecing methods to make prepieced segments. Join 2 or more strips, cut from the width of the fabric, on their long edges to make a strip unit. Press the seam in one direction (generally toward the darker fabric) and cut segments from the strip unit in the same way that you cut squares from a single strip of fabric. Align the seam line with a line on the ruler to make sure the cut ends are at right angles to the seam.

▲▽▲▽▲▽▲▽▲▽▲▽▲▽▲▽▲▽ **NOTE** ▽▲▽▲▽▲▽▲▽▲▽▲▽▲▽▲

The directions in this book deal primarily with rotary-cutting methods. If you are not comfortable with this method of cutting, you can make templates by following the rotary-cutting directions with a pencil and paper rather than a blade and fabric. Draw the pieces on graph paper using the measurements provided, then make your templates from your drawings. Remember, do not *add ¼"-wide seam allowances. Seam allowances are already included in the rotary-cutting measurements.*

▲▽▲▽▲▽▲▽▲▽▲▽▲▽▲▽▲▽▲▽▲▽▲▽▲▽▲▽▲▽▲▽▲▽▲▽▲▽

Machine Piecing

An accurate, consistent ¼"-wide seam allowance is the key to machine-piecing success. Some machines have a special foot that measures exactly ¼" from the center needle position to the edge of the presser foot. There are also specialty feet available at your sewing center as well as magnetic seam guides. (*Caution:* Do not use magnetic seam guides with computerized sewing machines!) If these options are not available to you, you can make a seam guide by building up a layer of tape ¼" away from the center needle position.

When checking your ¼"-wide seam allowances, make sure the stitching falls just inside the ¼" mark. I do this because the fold created by pressing the seams to one side takes up a small amount of fabric. If your seam allowances are too big, it could affect the block size. This can quickly add up to a measurable amount in blocks with many seams.

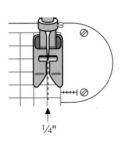

¼"

Making Half-Square Triangle Units

There are many quick methods for making half-square triangle units. My favorite is the grid method, using 2 pieces of fabric.

1. Use a fabric marker or pencil to mark a grid of squares on the wrong side of one fabric. Draw a diagonal line through each square as shown. Use a yellow or silver pencil to mark dark fabrics. Each pattern contains instructions for the required fabric size, the grid size, and the number of squares to draw.

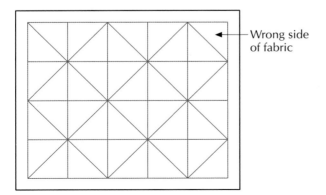

Wrong side of fabric

2. Layer the marked piece of fabric with another piece of fabric of the same size, right sides together. Pin the layers together in the triangle areas, away from the marked lines. Using a ¼"-wide seam allowance, stitch on each side of the diagonal lines. Follow the arrows for continuous sewing.

Start.

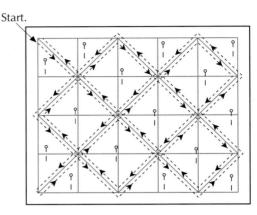

▲▽▲▽▲▽▲▽▲▽▲▽▲▽▲▽ **NOTE** ▽▲▽▲▽▲▽▲▽▲▽▲▽▲▽

If you do not have a ¼" foot for your sewing machine, mark the sewing lines on either side of the cutting lines with a pencil. Use a dashed line so you can easily see the difference between the cutting and sewing lines.

▽▲▽▲▽▲▽▲▽▲▽▲▽▲▽▲▽▲▽▲▽▲▽▲▽▲▽

3. Lightly press the sewn unit. Using a rotary cutter and mat, cut the squares apart on all horizontal and vertical lines. Then cut the squares on the diagonal line between the 2 rows of stitching. Press the seams of half-square triangle units as instructed for the quilt you are making. Trim the dog ears. Cut the required number of squares for the quilt you are making.

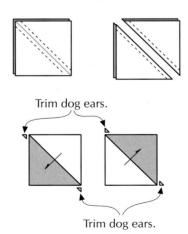

Trim dog ears.

Trim dog ears.

Pressing

Pressing is an important step in making your blocks and assembling your quilt. The general rule is to press seams toward the darker fabric to prevent the darker seam allowances from showing through the finished quilt. This rule is sometimes broken to make the construction of a block easier. Whenever possible, press seams that will meet at an intersection in opposite directions to keep the seams aligned as you sew.

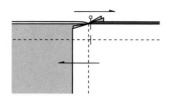

Press seam allowances as indicated by the arrows in the piecing diagrams.

Machine Appliqué

A little practice before you start your project will help you feel comfortable with this appliqué method. Familiarize yourself with your machine's satin-stitch variations. The manual is a good place to start. Follow the manufacturer's recommendations for setting thread tension, stitch length, and stitch width. Set the stitch width at ⅛" or slightly less, adjusting it to your taste.

Stitch a few samples on scrap fabric. Examine the samples for the following:

✳ Does the top thread lie flat on the fabric surface? If not, reduce the top thread tension.
✳ Does the bobbin thread show on top? If it does, reduce the top thread tension
✳ Do the top stitches lie very close to each other but not touch? If they touch or overlap, lengthen the stitch slightly; if they are too far apart, shorten the stitch length.

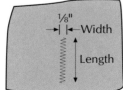

Note: The zigzag stitches have been lengthened for illustration purposes only.

Use one color throughout or change the top thread to match each color of appliqué fabric. If you adjust the stitch tension so that the bobbin thread does not show on top, you can use any thread color in the bobbin. However, if the bobbin thread does show on top, be sure to match it to the top thread.

Sew some samples on scrap fabric and make any needed adjustments. When your samples look good, try to stitch some wide and narrow curves. If you have a difficult time turning the fabric smoothly, reduce the presser-foot tension. If you cannot adjust the presser-foot tension on your machine, cover or drop the feed dogs, but remember that you are now controlling the stitch length.

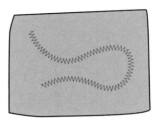

If none of these adjustments seem to help, you may need to use a stabilizer. There are many types of stabilizer available, such as tear-away and iron-on. Read the package information to determine which will suit your needs. Place the stabilizer on the wrong side of the fabric and repeat the sample stitching and machine adjustments until you are satisfied with the stitch quality.

Once you have your machine stitching properly, cut some easy shapes from scrap fabric and pin these to a larger scrap. Practice the actual appliqué stitch.

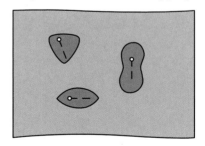

1. Position the appliqué under the presser foot so the right-hand, needle-down position falls just to the right of the appliqué without touching it.

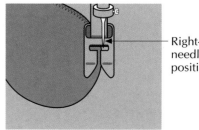

Right-hand, needle-down position

2. Place your hands on either side of the presser foot. Exert slight outward pressure with both hands, using your hands as a hoop to keep the fabric slightly taut and smooth under the presser foot.

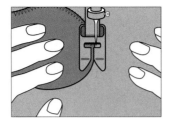

3. Start stitching slowly. As you sew, watch the outside edge of the appliqué and the right-hand, needle-down stroke. Keep the stitches as close to the edge as possible. You want to cover the outer edge of the appliqué with neat stitches without causing the edge to fray by stitching too close.

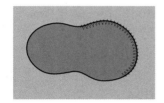

4. Use your hands in unison as you guide the stitching around the appliqué. When turning on an outside curve, move your right hand away from you and your left hand toward you, just as if your hands were on a steering wheel. On an inside curve, move your hands in the opposite direction.

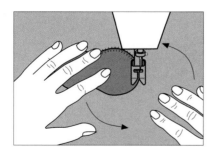

5. To end your stitching, take 2 stitches overlapping the beginning stitches and 2 stitches backward to lock the threads.

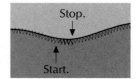

Corners

To turn on an outside corner:

1. Stitch to the corner and stop with the right-hand needle position on the outside of the appliqué.
2. Lift the presser foot and turn the background fabric so that the next side of the appliqué is in position. Turn the handwheel to raise the needle. Move the appliqué so that the left-hand needle position is directly under the previous line of stitching and the right-hand needle position is at the edge of the unstitched side of the appliqué.
3. Continue stitching.

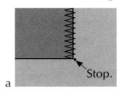
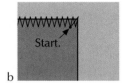

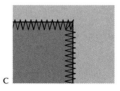

To turn on an inside corner:

1. Stitch to the corner and stop with the right-hand needle position in the corner on the outside of the appliqué.
2. Lift the presser foot and turn the background fabric so that the next side of the appliqué is in position. Turn the handwheel to raise the needle. Move the appliqué so that the left-hand needle position is slightly to the left of the previous stitches and the right-hand needle position will fall at the edge of the previous stitches.
3. Continue stitching.

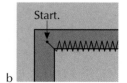

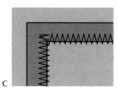

Curves

Curved areas present a slightly different problem. You will have to stop and pivot the fabric when stitching around severe curves. The amount of pivoting required depends on the tightness of the curve. You may be able to stitch around gentle curves without pivoting at all. The goal in pivoting is to turn the appliqué so that the stitches are always perpendicular to the outside edge. The stitches should not slant around a curve.

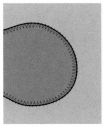 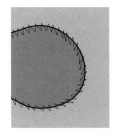

Right   Wrong

To turn on an inside curve:

1. Stop stitching with the needle down in the inside of the appliqué.
2. Lift the presser foot and pivot the appliqué so the next stitch will be perpendicular to the edge of the appliqué. Take a few stitches. Stop, pivot, and take another few stitches.
3. Continue stopping, pivoting, and stitching around the curved shape.

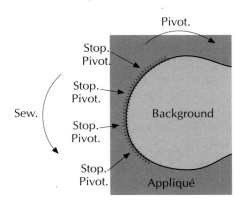

▲▽▲▽▲▽▲▽▲▽▲▽▲▽ **NOTE** ▽▲▽▲▽▲▽▲▽▲▽▲▽

The number of stitches you take between pivots depends on the severity of the curve.

▲▽▲▽▲▽▲▽▲▽▲▽▲▽▲▽▲▽▲▽▲▽▲▽▲▽▲▽

To turn on an outside curve:

1. Stop stitching with the needle down on the outside of the appliqué.
2. Lift the presser foot and pivot the appliqué so the next stitch will be perpendicular to the edge of the appliqué. Take a few stitches. Stop, pivot, and take another few stitches.
3. Continue stopping, pivoting, and stitching around the curved shape.

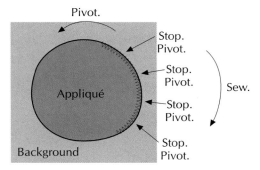

▲▽▲▽▲▽▲▽▲▽▲▽▲▽▲▽ **NOTE** ▽▲▽▲▽▲▽▲▽▲▽▲

If a few threads of the appliqué have frayed through the stitching, trim them closely with small scissors.

▲▽▲▽▲▽▲▽▲▽▲▽▲▽▲▽▲▽▲▽▲▽▲▽▲▽▲▽▲▽

Positioning Appliqués

To position appliqués on the background fabric, I use what I call "pin-through" templates. These templates consist of a full-size portion of the background block with the appliqué shapes cut out of the template in the proper position. Make pin-through templates from template plastic or heavy paper.

1. Trace the placement guide onto template plastic, including the corner squares and any center lines. Cut out only the appliqué shape.

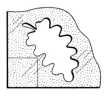

Template with leaf cut out and corner square marked

2. Lay the template on the appliqué block, aligning the corner square on the template with the corner square on the block.

3. Place the cutout fabric appliqué in the opening and pin in position before removing the template. Repeat with as many remaining corners as necessary to complete the appliqué.

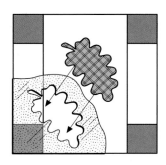

Another method that works well is to trace the pattern onto paper and draw the repeats until you have a diagram of the entire block. Then tape the drawing to a bright window or a light table, lay each background block over this pattern, and trace the design with a wash-out marker.

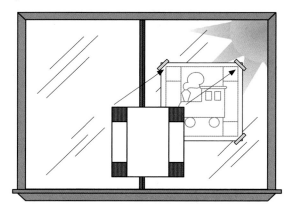

There are a number of ways to hold the appliqués in position as you stitch. Use the one that works best for you.

* Use quilters' pins or small silk pins, removing them as you sew.
* Baste the appliqué shapes by hand.
* Use a dab of wash-out fabric glue. Keep the glue away from the edges and any places where one appliqué will be sewn on top of another. The glue will gum up your needle if you sew through it.
* Fuse the appliqués to the background, then stitch around the edges.

Needle-Turn Appliqué

If you prefer to appliqué the pieces by hand, try this efficient method.

1. Make plastic or cardboard templates of the appliqué pieces. Trace the design onto the right side of the fabric.

2. Cut out the fabric piece, adding a ³⁄₁₆"-wide seam allowance all around.
3. Position the appliqué piece on the background fabric; pin or baste in place.
4. Starting on a straight edge, use the tip of the needle to gently turn under the seam allowance, about ½" at a time. Hold the turned seam allowance firmly between the thumb and first finger of your left hand (reverse if your are left-handed) as you stitch the appliqué to the background. Use a longer needle–a Sharp or a milliner's needle–to control the seam allowance and turn it under neatly.

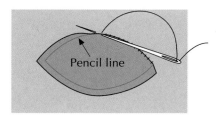

Pencil line

5. Tie a knot in a single strand of thread, approximately 18" long.
6. Hide the knot by slipping the needle into the seam allowance from the wrong side of the appliqué piece, bringing it out on the fold line.
7. Start the first stitch by moving the needle straight off the appliqué, inserting the needle into the background fabric. Let the needle travel under the background fabric, parallel to the edge of the appliqué, bringing it up about ⅛" away, along the pattern line.
8. As you bring the needle up, pierce the edge of the appliqué, catching only 1 or 2 threads of the folded edge.
9. Move the needle straight off the appliqué into the background fabric. Let your needle travel under the background, bring it up about ⅛" away, again catching the edge of the appliqué.
10. Give the thread a slight tug; continue stitching.

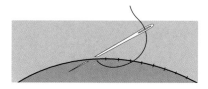

11. To end your stitching, pull the needle through to the wrong side. Take 2 small stitches behind the appliqué and knot the thread. Clip the thread tail.

ASSEMBLY AND FINISHING

Straight-Set Quilts

1. Arrange the blocks as indicated in each project.
2. Sew the blocks together in horizontal rows; press the seams toward the pieced blocks.
3. Sew the rows together, making sure to match the seams between blocks.

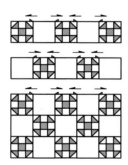

Press seams as indicated by arrows.

Adding Borders

Yardage requirements for the borders in this book are based on strips cut across the width of the fabric (crosswise grain), which are joined to get the required length. If you prefer borders without seams, you will need to purchase additional yardage and cut strips from the lengthwise grain to the required size.

To add straight-cut borders:

1. Measure the length of the quilt top through the center, not along one of the edges, and cut both side borders to this measurement, piecing strips as needed. Mark the center of the quilt top and the border strips, and pin the border strips to either

side of the quilt top at the center marks and ends, easing as necessary. Sew the border strips in place and press the seams toward the border.

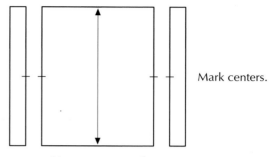

Measure center of quilt, top to bottom.

Mark centers.

2. Measure the width of the quilt, including the borders just added. Cut the top and bottom borders to this measurement, piecing strips as needed. Mark the center of the quilt top and bottom, and the centers of the border strips. Pin borders to the top and bottom edges of the quilt top, matching the center marks and ends, easing as necessary. Sew the border strips in place and press the seams toward the border.

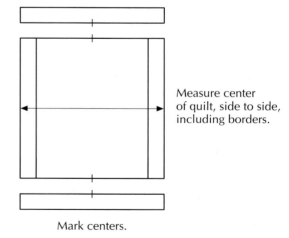

Measure center of quilt, side to side, including borders.

Mark centers.

Marking the Quilt

If you wish to mark specific quilting patterns, it is best to do so before layering the top, batting, and backing. Use a marking tool that is easy to see and easy to remove from your fabrics; test it on scraps if you are in doubt.

If you plan to stitch in-the-ditch or outline quilt, it's not necessary to mark the lines beforehand.

Preparing the Backing

Quilts consist of three layers: the top, batting, and backing. There are fabrics available on the market that measure 90" wide, and even 120" wide, that make nice seamless backings.

If you use standard 44"-wide fabric, you will need to join two or three lengths of fabric together to make a backing at least 4" larger than your quilt top. Remove the selvage edges before joining the back pieces and press the seams open to reduce bulk.

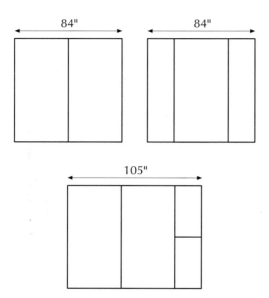

Selecting the Batting

Select a batting that fits your quilting plans. If you want to tie the quilt, choose a thick batting for a fluffy comforter look. If you plan to hand or machine quilt, a thinner batting is more appropriate and easier to stitch.

Take the batting out of its packaging a few hours before you assemble the layers to let it relax and lose some of the wrinkles. You can give the batting a quick fluff in the dryer, without heat, if desired.

Layering the Quilt

1. Spread the quilt back, wrong side up, on a clean, flat surface. If you are working on the carpet, pin the backing in place. Take care to keep it smooth, but do not stretch it. If you're working on a hard surface, use masking tape to hold the backing in place.

2. Spread the batting over the backing, smoothing out any wrinkles.

3. Place the pressed quilt top, right side up, on the batting and smooth into position. Take care not to shift the batting as you work. Keep the edges of the quilt top parallel to the edges of the backing. Check to see that the corners are square.

4. Baste the layers together, using needle and thread, rust-proof safety pins, or another basting method. Start in the center and move diagonally to the corners of the quilt top. Baste from the center outward to the 4 sides of the quilt top, then continue basting to form a grid of rows about 6" to 10" apart. Finish by basting around the edges. Use only light-colored thread for basting, because dark colors may rub off on your quilt top.

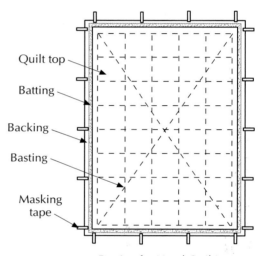

Basting for Hand Quilting

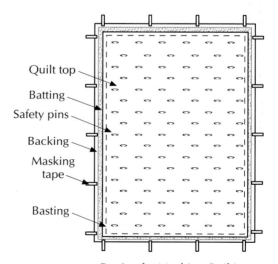

Basting for Machine Quilting

▲▼▲▼▲▼▲▼▲▼▲▼▲▼▲▼▲▼**TIP**▼▲▼▲▼▲▼▲▼▲▼▲▼▲▼

If you are working on the carpet, slide your rotary-cutting mat under the area you are basting, and move it around as needed for a firm surface under the layers.

Binding the Quilt

Cut 2½"-wide strips across the width of the fabric for straight-grain, French double-fold binding. You will need enough strips to go around all four sides of the quilt and an additional 10" to 15" for seams and mitered corners.

Preparing the Binding

1. Sew all the strips together by placing the end of one strip at right angles to the next and sewing diagonally across the corner. Trim the excess fabric and press the seams open to reduce bulk.

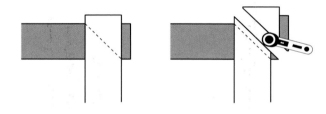

2. Fold the entire strip in half lengthwise, wrong sides together, and press.

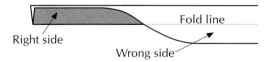

Attaching the Binding

1. Trim batting and backing even with the quilt top.
2. Start on one side of the quilt (not in a corner) and match the raw edges of the binding with the raw edges of the quilt top. Leaving the first 10" of binding unsewn, stitch the binding in place using

a ¼"-wide seam allowance. Stop stitching ¼" from the corner of the quilt and backstitch once. Clip the thread.

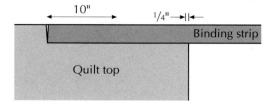

3. Turn the quilt so you will be stitching down the next side and fold the binding up and away from the quilt. This will form a 45°-angle fold in the binding.

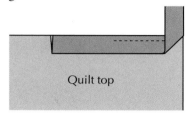

4. Keeping the folded angle in place, bring the binding back down over itself, parallel with the next edge of the quilt to be sewn.

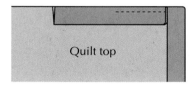

5. You will be able to feel the 45° fold now hidden by the binding. Start stitching where this fold bisects the ¼" seam line for the next seam; backstitch to secure, then continue sewing the seam.

6. Continue to sew the binding to the quilt edge, making the folded miters at each corner, until you are within 10" of your starting point.

7. Remove the quilt from the sewing machine and lay the unsewn section on a flat surface. Fold the unsewn binding ends back on themselves so that they just meet in the middle over the unsewn area of the quilt top; finger-press both bindings to mark this junction. This will make an X on the binding when unfolded.

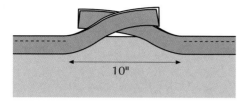

10"

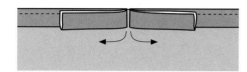

8. Unfold both sides of the bindings and match the centers of the pressed Xs. Sew across the intersection as when sewing the strips together. Trim the excess fabric and press the seam open. Finish stitching the binding to the quilt edge.

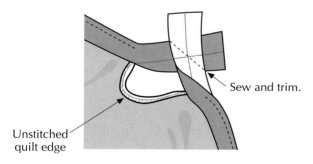

Sew and trim.

Unstitched quilt edge

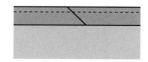

9. Press the binding away from the quilt top on all sides.

10. Fold the binding over the raw edges of the quilt to the back. Blindstitch in place, covering the machine stitching. As you fold the binding around the corner, a miter will form automatically.

Quilt back

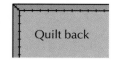

Quilt back

Signing the Quilt

At the very least, sign your quilt with your full name and the date. If the quilt is a gift, a personal sentiment is appropriate. Write the full names of both the giver and the recipient. For example:

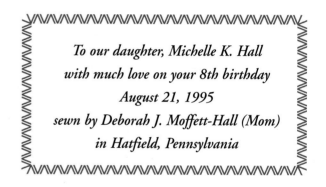

To our daughter, Michelle K. Hall
with much love on your 8th birthday
August 21, 1995
sewn by Deborah J. Moffett-Hall (Mom)
in Hatfield, Pennsylvania

The label above gives future generations much more information than this:

Happy Birthday, Shelly!
With love, Mom.

I admit that the first version seems stilted and formal and the second feels more natural, but later, when Michelle's great-grandchildren are sorting through all the stuff in the attic, the first version will answer all their questions.

Sister's Choice—Ring-a-Rosy, blocks pieced by Beth G. Hertz, appliquéd and quilted by Deborah J. Moffett-Hall, April 1995, Hatfield, Pennsylvania, 46" x 58". My friend Beth selected this pattern to make a quilt for her oldest daughter, Colleen. Since Colleen likes bright colors and the latest fashions, a contemporary print in raspberry and periwinkle seemed the perfect starting point. Directions begin on page 34.

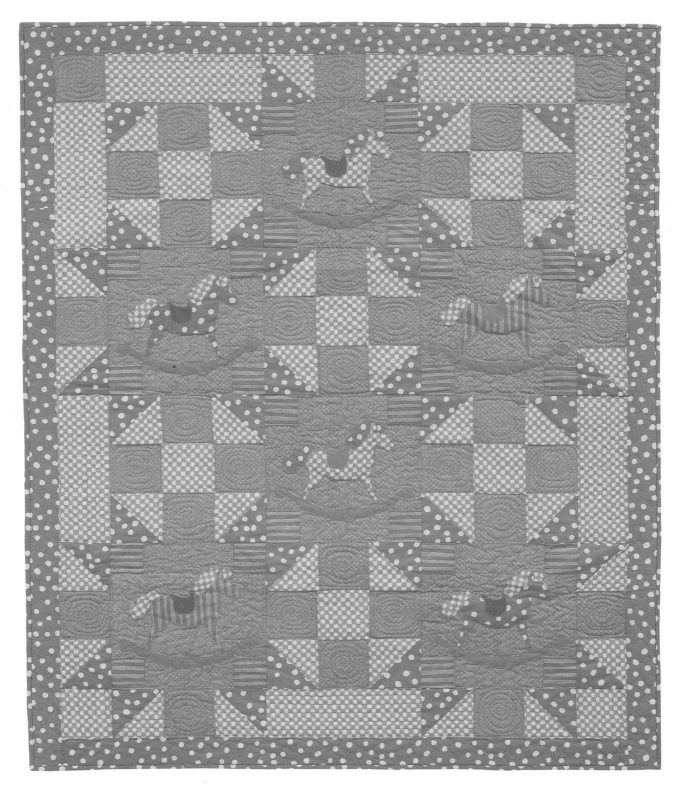

Shoofly—Rock-a-Bye by Deborah J. Moffett-Hall, October 1994, Hatfield, Pennsylvania, 49" x 61". Baby quilts offer the perfect opportunity to play with all the wonderful, fun prints found in fabric shops. These bright and energetic rocking horses look as if they pranced off a merry-go-round. Directions begin on page 25. Take a look at "Churn Dash—Rock-a-Bye" (opposite) to see what a difference fabric choice can make.

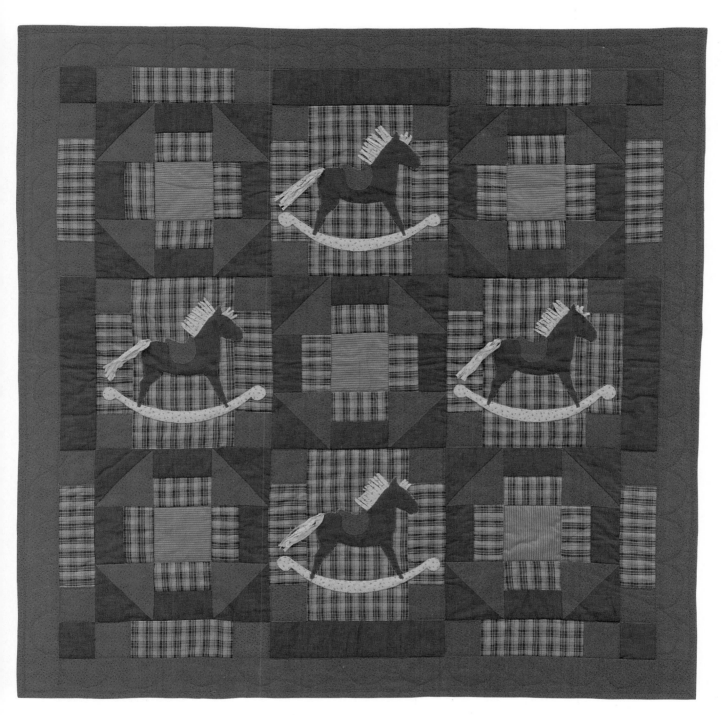

Churn Dash—Rock-a-Bye by Deborah J. Moffett-Hall, October 1994, Hatfield, Pennsylvania, 46" x 46". Homespun plaids and stripes give these rocking horses a country feel. The clipped manes and tails are reminiscent of the string tails found on antique wooden rocking horses. Directions begin on page 29.

Broken Wheel–Choo-Choo by Deborah J. Moffett-Hall, September 1994, Hatfield, Pennsylvania, 44" x 56". I love making baby quilts. They stitch up quickly and are much-appreciated gifts. I plan to personalize the engines by embroidering the baby's name under the windows. To make this quilt extra special, add the baby's birth date, weight, hometown, and the parents' names to the other engines. Directions begin on the opposite page.

Broken Wheel—Choo-Choo

Finished Quilt Size: 44" x 56" ▪ Finished Block Size: 12" ▪ Color photo opposite.

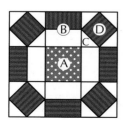

Broken Wheel
Make 6.

Choo-Choo
Make 6.

Blue stripe

Tan

Red star print

Red solid

Brown print

Yellow solid

21

Materials: 44"-wide fabric

1⅝ yds.   blue stripe for pieced blocks, appliqués, outer border, and binding
1½ yds.   tan for pieced blocks
¾ yd.   red star print for pieced blocks and inner border
¼ yd.   red solid for engines
⅛ yd.   brown print for smoke
⅛ yd.   yellow solid for engine windows
3½ yds.   for backing

Cutting

Cut all strips across the width of the fabric.

From the blue stripe, cut:

3 strips, each 2½" x 42", for pieced blocks (B)
2 strips, each 3⅜" x 42"
  • crosscut into 24 squares, each 3⅜" x 3⅜", for blocks (D)
2 strips, each 3" x 42", for appliqué blocks
5 strips, each 2½" x 42", for outer borders
5 strips, each 2½" x 42", for binding
1 strip, ½" x 30"
  • crosscut into 6 rectangles, each 4½" long. Round the corners with roof Template 4.
6 of Template 2 for smokestacks
12 of Template 5 for wheels

From the tan fabric, cut:

3 strips, each 2½" x 42", for pieced blocks (B)
4 strips, each 2⅞" x 42"
  • crosscut into 48 squres, each 2⅞" x 2⅞". Cut the squares once diagonally to yield 96 triangles for pieced blocks (C).
2 strips, each 7½" x 42"
  • crosscut into 6 rectangles, each 7½" x 12½", for appliqué blocks
1 strip, 7½" x 42", for appliqué blocks

From the red star print, cut:

1 strip, 4½" x 42"
  • crosscut into 6 squares, each 4½" x 4½", for pieced blocks (A)
5 strips, each 2½" x 42", for inner border

From the red solid, cut:

3 of Template 3 for right-facing engine
3 of Template 3 reversed for left-facing engine

From the brown print, cut:

3 of Template 1 for right-facing smoke cloud
3 of Template 1 reversed for left-facing smoke cloud

From the yellow solid, cut:

1 strip, 1½" x 12"
  • crosscut into 12 rectangles, each 1½" x 1", for engine windows

Assembling the Broken Wheel Blocks

1. Sew a 2½"-wide tan strip to a 2½"-wide blue strip to make a strip unit as shown. Cut the strip units into a total of 24 segments, each 4½" wide.

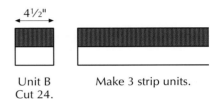

Unit B
Cut 24.   Make 3 strip units.

2. Sew 2 tan triangles (C) to opposite sides of a blue square (D). Add 2 tan triangles to the remaining sides. Trim the dog ears.

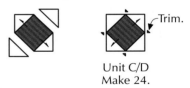

Unit C/D
Make 24.

3. Assemble the units following the piecing diagram to make a Broken Wheel block.

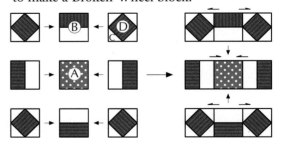

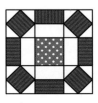

Make 6.

Assembling the Appliqué Blocks

1. Sew a 3"-wide blue strip to each side of a 7½" x 42" tan strip to make a strip unit. Cut the strip unit into 12 segments, each 3" wide. To make an appliqué block, sew 2 segments to opposite sides of a 7½" x 12½" tan rectangle.

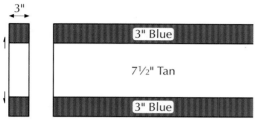

Cut 12.   Make 1 strip unit.

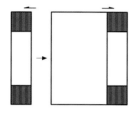

Make 6.

2. Refer to the Choo-Choo placement guide on page 24 to position the appliqué pieces on the appliqué blocks. Make 3 right-facing and 3 left-facing engines. Stitch in place and press the completed blocks.

Assembling and Finishing the Quilt

1. Arrange the Broken Wheel blocks and appliqué blocks in horizontal rows, alternating the blocks as shown in the quilt plan on page 21.

2. Sew the blocks together in horizontal rows, pressing the seams toward the appliqué blocks. Join the rows, matching the seams between the blocks.

3. Add the 2½"-wide red star print inner border, referring to "Straight-Cut Borders" on page 13. Repeat with the 2½"-wide blue stripe outer border.

4. Layer the quilt top, batting, and backing; baste.

5. Quilt as desired or follow the quilting suggestion below. Bind the edges.

6. Sign your quilt.

Quilting Suggestion

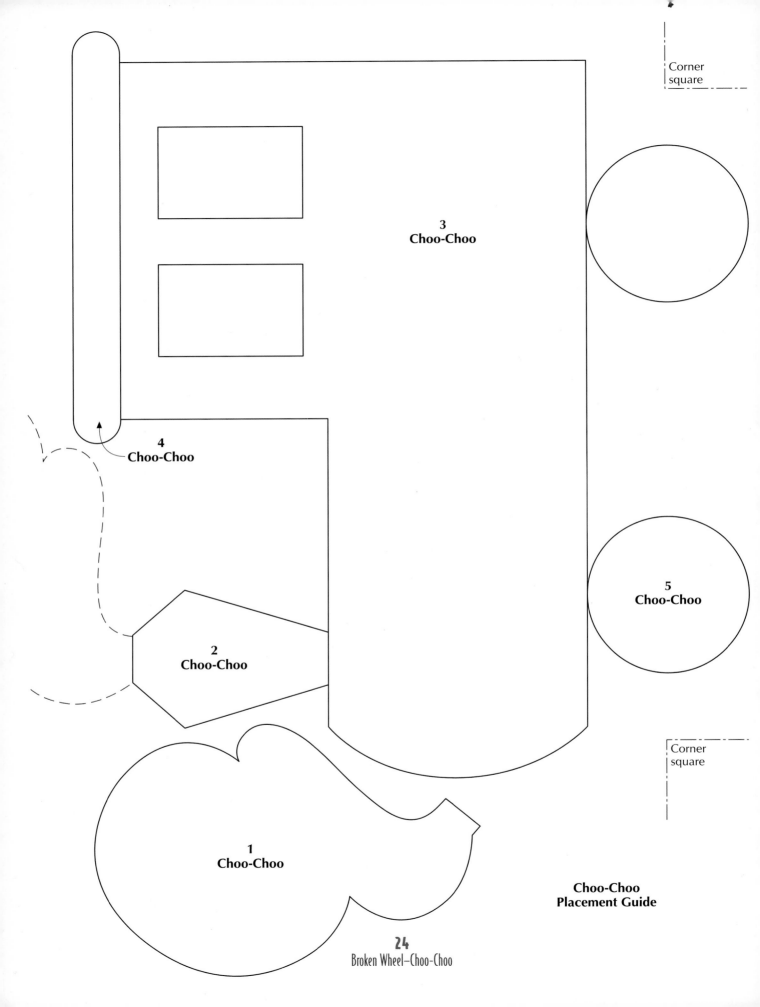

Corner
square

**3
Choo-Choo**

**4
Choo-Choo**

**5
Choo-Choo**

**2
Choo-Choo**

Corner
square

**Choo-Choo
Placement Guide**

**1
Choo-Choo**

Shoofly–Rock-a-Bye

Finished Quilt Size: 49" x 61" • Finished Block Size: 12" • Color photo on page 18.

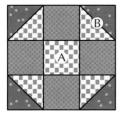

Shoofly
Make 6.

Rock-a-Bye
Make 6.

Blue-and-pink dot		Blue-and-pink stripe
Blue-and-pink check		Blue solid
Pink check		Pink solid

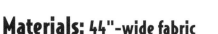

Materials: 44"-wide fabric

1¾ yds.   blue-and-pink dot for pieced blocks, appliqués, pieced border, outer border, and binding

1⅜ yds.   blue-and-pink check for pieced and appliqué blocks and pieced border

1¼ yds.   pink check for pieced blocks, appliqués, and pieced border

½ yd.   blue-and-pink stripe for pieced and appliqué blocks and appliqués

¼ yd.   blue solid for appliqués

⅛ yd.   pink solid for appliqués

3½ yds.   for backing

Cutting

Cut all strips across the width of the fabric.

From the blue-and-pink dot, cut:
1 piece, 22" x 28", for half-square triangle units (B)
6 strips, each 3" x 42", for outer border
6 strips, each 2½" x 42", for binding
2 of Template 2 for manes
2 of Template 3 for tails
2 of Template 4 for ponies

From the blue-and-pink check, cut:
4 strips, each 4½" x 42"
  • cut 2 smaller strips, each 4½" x 28", from 2 of the strips. Cut the remainder of the strips into 21 squares, each 4½" x 4½", for pieced blocks (A) and pieced border.
1 strip, 7½" x 42" for appliqué blocks
2 strips, each 7½" x 42"
  • crosscut into 6 rectangles, each 7½" x 12½", for appliqué blocks

From the pink check, cut:
1 piece, 22" x 28", for half-square triangle units (B)
1 strip, 4½" x 42"
  • cut into 1 piece, 4½" x 28", and 2 squares, each 4½" x 4½" for pieced blocks and pieced border
1 strip, 12½" x 42"
  • crosscut into 7 strips, each 4½" x 12½", for pieced border
4 of Template 2 for manes
4 of Template 3 for tails
2 of Template 4 for ponies

From the blue-and-pink stripe, cut:
2 strips, each 3" x 42", for appliqué blocks
2 of Template 4 for ponies

From the blue solid, cut:
6 of Template 1 for rockers
2 of Template 5 for saddles

From the pink solid, cut:
4 of Template 5 for saddles

Assembling the Shoofly Blocks

1. Refer to "Making Half-Square Triangle Units" on page 8. Using the 22" x 28" pieces of pink check and blue-and-pink dot, mark a grid of 4⅞" squares, 5 across and 4 down. Make 38 half-square triangle units. Press the seams toward the blue-and-pink dot triangles.

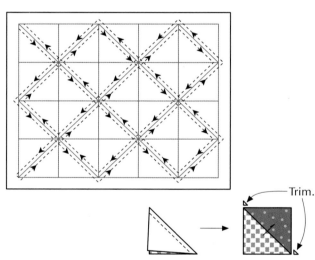

Unit B
Make 38.

2. Sew a 4½" x 28" blue-and-pink check strip to each side of a 4½" x 28" pink-check strip to make a strip unit as shown. Cut the strip unit into 6 segments, each 4½" wide.

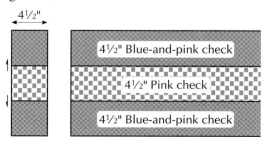

Cut 6.   Make 1 strip unit.

3. Sew 2 half-square triangle units and 1 blue-and-pink check square together. Be sure to orient the half-square triangle units as shown.

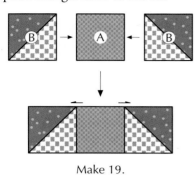

Make 19.

4. Assemble segments following the piecing diagram to complete the Shoofly block.

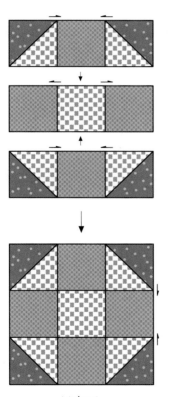

Make 6.

Assembling the Appliqué Blocks

1. Sew a 3" x 42" strip of blue-and-pink stripe to each side of a 7½" x 42" blue-and-pink check strip to make a strip unit as shown. Cut the strip unit into 12 segments, each 3" wide. Sew 2 segments to opposite sides of a 7½" x 12½" blue-and-pink check rectangle to make an appliqué block.

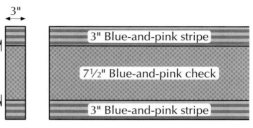

3"

3" Blue-and-pink stripe

7½" Blue-and-pink check

3" Blue-and-pink stripe

Cut 12.   Make 1 strip unit.

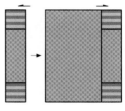

Make 6.

2. Refer to the Rock-a-Bye placement guide on page 33 to position the following appliqué pieces:
- 2 blue-dot ponies, each with a pink-check mane and tail and a pink-solid saddle
- 2 blue-and-pink stripe ponies, each with a pink-check mane and tail; 1 with a blue saddle and 1 with a pink saddle
- 2 pink-check ponies, each with blue-dot mane and tail; 1 with a blue saddle and 1 with a pink saddle

Stitch the appliqués in place and press the completed block.

Assembling and Finishing the Quilt

1. Arrange the Shoofly and appliqué blocks in horizontal rows, alternating the blocks as shown in the quilt plan on page 25.
2. Sew the blocks together in horizontal rows, pressing the seams toward the appliqué blocks. Join the rows, making sure to match the seams between the blocks.
3. To make the pieced borders, join the remaining half-square triangle units and 4½" x 12½" pink-check strips, adding the 4½" squares to the top and bottom borders as shown.

Right Border

Left Border

Top Border

Bottom Border

4. Sew the left and right borders to the quilt top, then add the top and bottom borders. Be sure to orient the pink-and-blue polka dot triangles as shown in the quilt plan.
5. Add the 3"-wide outer border, referring to "Straight-Cut Borders" on page 13.
6. Layer the quilt top, batting, and backing; baste.
7. Quilt as desired, or follow the quilting suggestion below. Bind the edges.
8. Sign your quilt.

Quilting Suggestion

Churn Dash–Rock-a-Bye

Finished Quilt Size: 46" x 46" • Finished Block Size: 12" • Color photo on page 19.

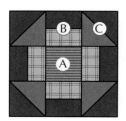

Churn Dash
Make 5.

Rock-a-Bye
Make 4.

Red print   Red stripe

Plaid   Tan print

Blue solid

29

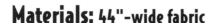

Materials: 44"-wide fabric

1⅝ yds. red print for pieced and appliqué blocks, appliqués, outer border, and binding
1¼ yds. plaid for pieced and appliqué blocks
1 yd. blue solid for pieced blocks, appliqués, and pieced border
¼ yd. red stripe for pieced blocks
¼ yd. tan print for appliqués
2¾ yds. for backing

Cutting

Cut all strips across the width of the fabric.

From the red print, cut:

2 strips, each 3" x 18", for appliqué blocks and pieced border
2 strips, each 3" x 42", for appliqué blocks and pieced border
5 strips, each 3" x 42", for outer border
1 piece, 11" x 27", for half-square triangle units (C)
5 strips, each 2½" x 42", for binding
4 of Template 5 for saddles

From the plaid, cut:

1 strip, 2½" x 21", for pieced blocks (B)
2 strips, each 2½" x 42", for pieced blocks (B)
1 strip, 7½" x 18", for appliqué blocks and pieced border
1 strip, 7½" x 42", for appliqué blocks and pieced border
1 strip, 12½" x 42"
  • crosscut into 4 rectangles, each 7½" x 12½", for appliqué blocks

From the blue solid, cut:

1 strip, 2½" x 21", for pieced blocks (B)
2 strips, each 2½" x 42", for pieced blocks (B)
2 strips, each 3" x 42"
  • crosscut into 4 pieces, each 3" x 12½". Cut 4 squares, each 3" x 3", for the pieced border, from the remainder of the strips.
1 piece, 11" x 27", for half-square triangle units (C)
4 of Template 4 for ponies

From the red stripe, cut:

5 squares, each 4½" x 4½", for pieced blocks (A)

From the tan print, cut:

4 rectangles, each 1½" x 3", for three-dimensional manes (or Template 2)
4 rectangles, each 3" x 4", for three-dimensional tails (or Template 3)
4 of Template 1 for rockers

▽△▽△▽△▽△▽△▽△▽△ **NOTE** ▽△▽△▽△▽△▽△▽△▽△▽

The ponies' tails and manes in this quilt are three-dimensional. The tails and manes in the "Shoofly—Rock-a-Bye" quilt on page 25 are made from templates and are not three-dimensional. Choose whichever method you prefer.

▽△▽△▽△▽△▽△▽△▽△▽△▽△▽△▽△▽△▽△▽△▽△▽△▽

Assembling the Churn Dash Blocks

1. Sew a 2½" x 42" plaid strip to a 2½" x 42" blue strip to make a strip unit as shown. Repeat with 2½" x 21" plaid and blue strips. Cut the strip units into a total of 20 segments, each 4½" wide.

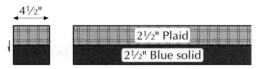

4½"

2½" Plaid
2½" Blue solid

Cut 20.   Make 2 strip units 42" long.
                 Make 1 strip unit 21" long.

2. Refer to "Making Half-Square Triangle Units" on page 8. Using the 11" x 27" pieces of blue solid and red print, mark a grid of 4⅞" squares, 5 across and 2 down. Make 20 half-square triangle units. Press the seams toward the blue triangles.

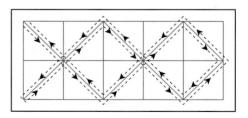

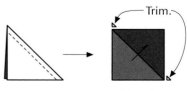

Trim.

Unit C
Make 20.

3. Assemble the units following the piecing diagram to make a Churn Dash block.

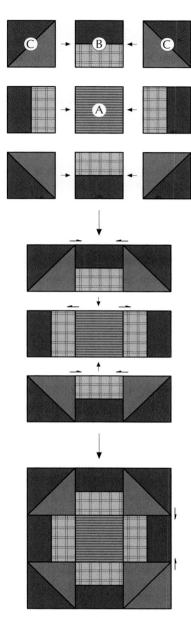

Make 5.

Assembling the Appliqué Blocks

1. Sew a 3" x 42" red print strip to each side of the 7½" x 42" plaid strip to make a strip unit as shown above right. Repeat with the 3" x 18" red print strips and 7½" x 18" plaid strip to make a shorter strip unit. Cut the strip units into a total of 16 segments, each 3" wide. Sew 2 segments to opposite sides of a 7½" x 12½" plaid rectangle to make an appliqué block. Reserve the remaining 8 segments for the pieced border.

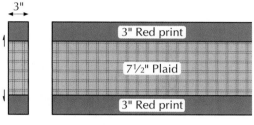

Cut 16.

Make 1 strip unit 42" long.
Make 1 strip unit 18" long.

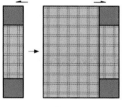

Make 4.

2. Refer to the Rock-a-Bye placement guide on page 33 to position the appliqué pieces on the appliqué block. Use templates to make tails and manes, or follow steps 3 and 4 below for making three-dimensional tails and manes. Stitch in place and press the completed blocks.

3. To make a tail, make ³⁄₁₆"-wide cuts in a 3" x 4" tan rectangle as shown, stopping ¼" from one end. Roll the end and secure at the rear end of the horse before appliquéing the body in place.

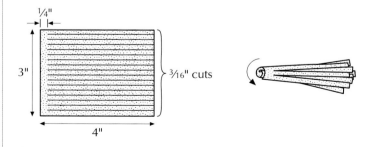

4. To make the mane, make ⅛"-wide cuts in a 1½" x 3" tan rectangle as shown, stopping ¼" from one end. Baste the mane in place, placing about ¾" to 1" of the mane in front of the ear and the rest behind the ear.

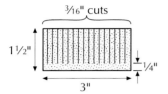

Assembling and Finishing the Quilt

1. Arrange the Churn Dash blocks and appliqué blocks in horizontal rows, alternating the blocks as shown in the quilt plan on page 29.
2. Sew the blocks together in horizontal rows, pressing the seams toward the Churn Dash blocks. Join the rows, matching the seams between the blocks.
3. Sew a 3" x 12½" blue solid strip between 2 red-plaid-red segments to make a pieced border strip.

Make 4.

4. Sew 2 borders to opposite sides of the quilt top. Press the seams toward the pieced border. Sew a 3" blue square to each end of the remaining pieced borders. Join these to the top and bottom edges of the quilt top. Press seams toward pieced border.

5. Add the 3"-wide outer border, referring to "Straight-Cut Borders" on page 13.
6. Layer the quilt top, batting, and backing; baste.
7. Quilt as desired, or follow the quilting suggestion below. Bind the edges.
8. Sign your quilt.

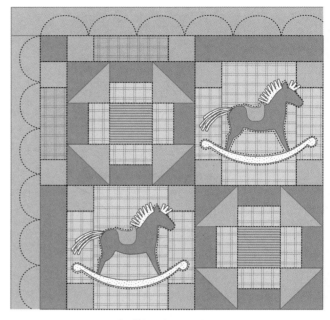

Quilting Suggestion

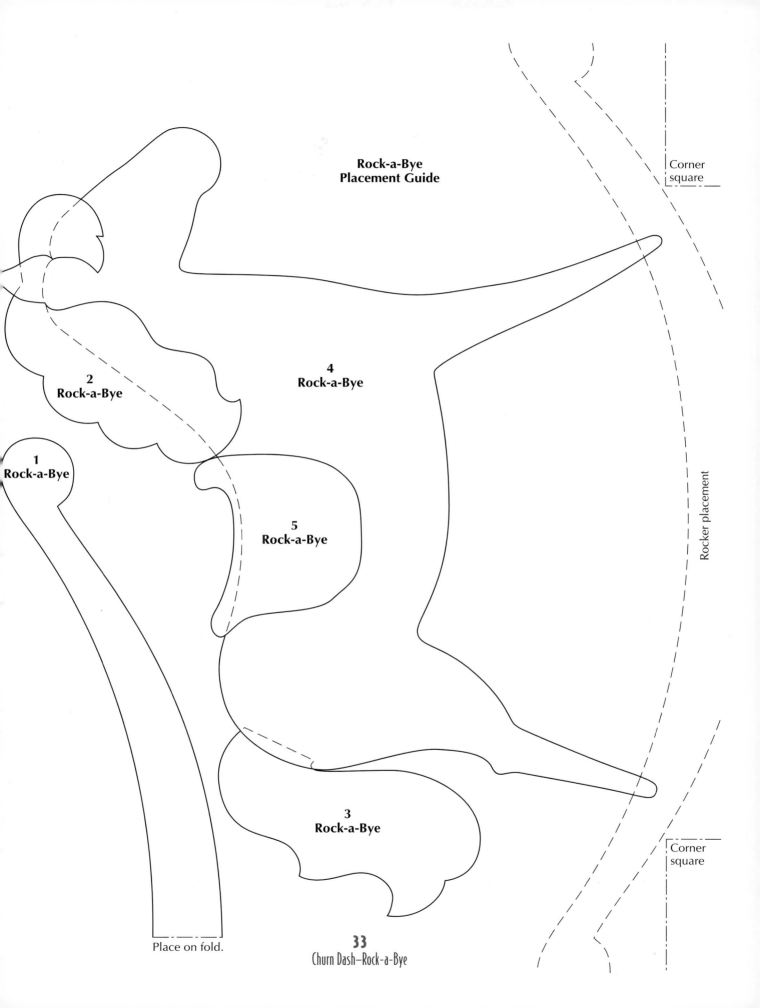

**Rock-a-Bye
Placement Guide**

Corner
square

**2
Rock-a-Bye**

**4
Rock-a-Bye**

**1
Rock-a-Bye**

**5
Rock-a-Bye**

Rocker placement

**3
Rock-a-Bye**

Corner
square

Place on fold.

33
Churn Dash–Rock-a-Bye

Sister's Choice—Ring-a-Rosy

Finished Quilt Size: 46" x 58" • Finished Block Size: 12" • Color photo on page 17.

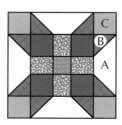

Sister's Choice
Make 6.

Ring-a-Rosy
Make 6.

☐ White solid	▦ Green solid
▦ Multicolor print	▦ Mauve print
▦ Blue print	▦ Blue solid

34

Materials: 44"-wide fabric

1¾ yds. white solid for pieced and appliqué blocks and pieced border
1½ yds. multicolor print for pieced and appliqué blocks, appliqués, and border
⅞ yd. blue print for pieced blocks, pieced border, and binding
¾ yd. green solid for pieced blocks, pieced border, and appliqués
½ yd. mauve print for pieced blocks and appliqués
⅜ yd. blue solid for pieced blocks
3½ yds. backing fabric

Cutting

Cut all strips across the width of the fabric.

From the white solid, cut:

5 strips, each 3" x 42", for pieced blocks (A)
1 strip, 7½" x 42", for appliqué blocks and pieced border
1 strip, 7½" x 21", for appliqué blocks and pieced border
2 strips, each 12½" x 42"
  • crosscut into 6 rectangles, each 7½" x 12½", for appliqué blocks

From the multicolor print, cut:

1 strip, 2½" x 42", for pieced blocks
10 strips, each 3" x 42", for pieced and appliqué blocks, pieced borders, and outer border
2 squares, each 3" x 3", for pieced border
24 of Template 3 for flower center

From the blue print, cut:

3 strips, each 3⅜"
  • crosscut into 31 squares, each 3⅜" x 3⅜". Cut the squares once diagonally to yield 62 triangles for pieced blocks (B).
5 strips, each 2½" x 42", for binding

From the green solid, cut:

3 strips, each 3" x 42"
  • crosscut into 40 squares, each 3" x 3", for pieced blocks (C) and pieced borders
48 of Template 1 for leaves

From the mauve print, cut:

1 strip, 2½" x 21", for pieced blocks
24 of Template 2 for flowers

From the blue solid, cut:

2 strips, each 3" x 42", for pieced blocks

Assembling the Sister's Choice Blocks

1. Cut one of the 3" x 42" multicolor print strips in half to make 2 strips, each 3" x 21". Sew a half strip to each side of the 2½" x 21" mauve strip to make a strip unit as shown. Cut the strip unit into 6 segments, each 2½" wide.

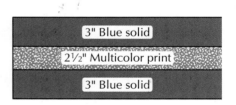

Cut 6.   Make 1 strip unit 21" long.

2. Sew a 3" x 42" blue solid strip to each side of a 2½" x 42" multicolor print strip to make a strip unit as shown. Cut the strip unit into 12 segments, each 3" wide.

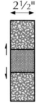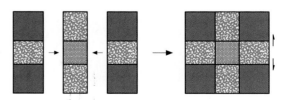

Cut 12.   Make 1 strip unit 42" long.

3. Sew the segments from steps 1 and 2 together to make a nine-patch unit.

Make 6.

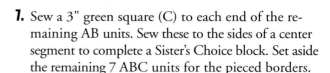

4. Make a plastic template of Template A on page 38. Place the plastic template at one end of a 3"-wide white strip. Use a pencil to mark the sides of the template and cut with scissors, or align a ruler with the edge of the template and cut along the edge of the ruler with your rotary cutter. Rotate the template along the strip as you cut the pieces. You should be able to cut 7 of piece A from each 42"-long strip.

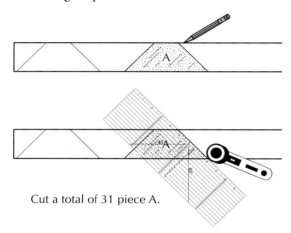

Cut a total of 31 piece A.

5. Sew 2 blue print triangles (B) to the sides of a white piece A. Trim the dog ears.

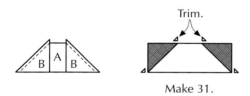

Make 31.

6. Sew an AB unit to the top and bottom of a nine-patch unit to make the center segment.

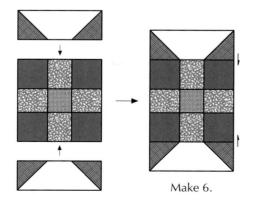

Make 6.

7. Sew a 3" green square (C) to each end of the remaining AB units. Sew these to the sides of a center segment to complete a Sister's Choice block. Set aside the remaining 7 ABC units for the pieced borders.

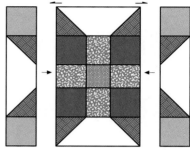

Make 19.

Make 6.

Assembling the Appliqué Block

1. Sew a 3" x 42" multicolor print strip to each side of a 7½" x 42" white strip to make a strip unit as shown. Cut one 3"-wide multicolor strip in half. Sew a half strip to each side of a 7½" x 21" white strip. Cut the strip units into a total of 19 segments, each 3" wide. Sew 2 segments to opposite sides of a 7½" x 12½" white rectangle to make an appliqué block. Set aside the remaining 7 segments for the pieced borders.

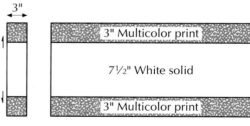

3"

3" Multicolor print

7½" White solid

3" Multicolor print

Cut 19.   Make 1 strip unit 42" long.
Make 1 strip unit 21" long.

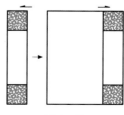

Make 6.

2. Refer to the Ring-a-Rosy placement guide on page 68 to position the appliqué pieces on the appliqué blocks. Stitch in place and press the completed blocks.

Assembling and Finishing the Quilt

1. Arrange the Sister's Choice and appliqué blocks in horizontal rows, alternating the blocks as shown in the quilt plan on page 34.
2. Sew the blocks together in horizontal rows, pressing the seams toward the Sister's Choice blocks. Join the rows, making sure to match the seams between the blocks.
3. Sew the remaining units together as shown to make the pieced border strips. Sew the left and right border strips to the quilt top. Sew a 3" green square to each end of the top border strip; add to the top edge. Sew a 3" multicolor print square to each end of the bottom border strip; add to bottom edge. Press the seams toward the border.

4. Add the 3"-wide outer border strips, referring to "Straight-Cut Borders" on page 13.
5. Layer the quilt top, batting, and backing; baste.
6. Quilt as desired, or follow the quilting suggestion below. Bind the edges.
7. Sign your quilt.

Quilting Suggestion

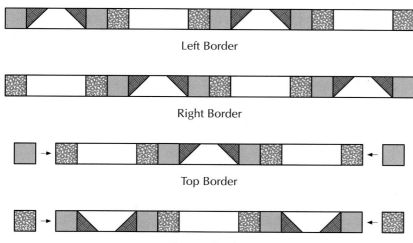

Left Border

Right Border

Top Border

Bottom Border

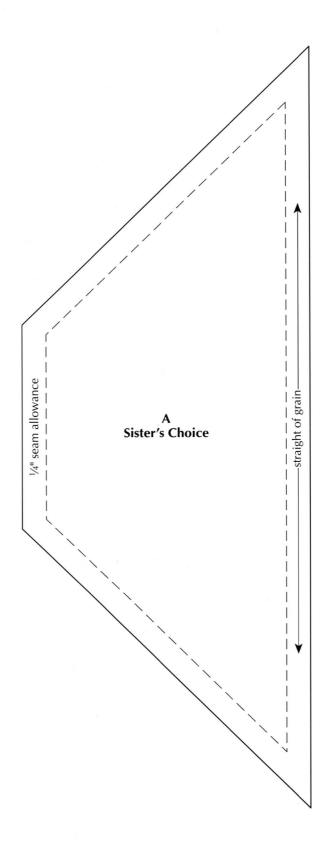

A
Sister's Choice

¼" seam allowance

straight of grain

Ohio Star–Balloons and Bows

Finished Quilt Size: 64" x 88" • Finished Block Size: 12" • Color photo on page 69.

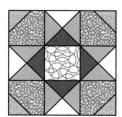

Ohio Star
Make 12.

Balloons and Bows
Make 12.

☐ White (W)			☐ Pink print (Pk)
☐ Floral print			☐ Green print
☐ Balloon print			☐ Purple print (Pr)
☐ Multicolor print			☐ Blue print (B)

Materials: 44"-wide fabric

2⅛ yds. white for pieced and appliqué blocks and inner-border triangles

2 yds. floral print for pieced blocks and inner border

1½ yds. balloon print for pieced blocks and outer border

1¼ yds. multicolor print for pieced blocks, balloons, and binding

1 yd. pink print for pieced and appliqué blocks and balloons

⅝ yd. green print for the pieced blocks, balloons, and bows

⅝ yd. purple print for the pieced blocks, balloons, and bows

⅝ yd. blue print for the pieced blocks, balloons, and bows

⅛ yd. light green for bow ends and centers

⅛ yd. dark purple for bow ends and centers

⅛ yd. dark blue for bow ends and centers

5½ yds. for backing

Cutting

Cut all strips across the width of the fabric.

From the white fabric, cut:
2 strips, each 5¼" x 42"
- crosscut into 12 squares, each 5¼" x 5¼". Cut the squares twice diagonally to yield 48 triangles for pieced blocks (B).

2 strips, each 7½" x 42", for appliqué blocks

3 strips, each 12½" x 42"
- crosscut into 12 rectangles, each 7½" x 12½", for appliqué blocks

1 strip, 3⅜" x 42"
- crosscut into 5 squares, each 3⅜" x 3⅜". Cut the squares once diagonally to yield 10 triangles for the inner border.

From the floral print, cut:
6 strips, each 4½" x 42"
- crosscut into 48 squares, each 4½" x 4½". Use the Cut-off Template A on page 68 to remove 1 corner from each square (C).

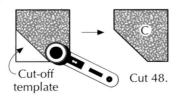

Cut-off template

C

Cut 48.

8 strips, each 4½" x 42", for inner border

From the balloon print, cut:
2 strips, each 4½" x 42"
- crosscut into 12 squares, each 4½" x 4½", for pieced blocks (A)

8 strips, each 4½" x 42", for outer border

From the multicolor print, cut:
2 strips, each 3⅜" x 42"
- crosscut into 24 squares, each 3⅜" x 3⅜". Cut the squares once diagonally to yield 48 triangles for pieced blocks (D).

8 strips, each 2½" x 42", for binding

12 of Template 1 for balloons

From the pink print, cut:
2 strips, each 5¼" x 42"
- crosscut into 9 squares, each 5¼" x 5¼". Cut the squares twice diagonally to yield 36 triangles for pieced blocks (B).

4 strips, each 3" x 42", for appliqué blocks

5 of Template 1 for balloons

From the green print, cut:
2 strips, each 5¼" x 42"
- crosscut into 9 squares, each 5¼" x 5¼". Cut the squares twice diagonally to yield 36 triangles for pieced blocks (B).

4 of Template 1 for balloons

4 of Template 3 for bows

From the purple print, cut:
2 strips, each 5¼" x 42"
- crosscut into 9 squares, each 5¼" x 5¼". Cut the squares twice diagonally to yield 36 triangles for pieced blocks (B).

8 of Template 1 for balloons

4 of Template 3 for bows

From the blue print, cut:
2 strips, each 5¼" x 42"
- crosscut into 9 squares, each 5¼" x 5¼". Cut the squares twice diagonally to yield 36 triangles for pieced blocks (B).

7 of Template 1 for balloons

4 of Template 3 for bows

From the light green, cut:
8 of Template 2 for bow ends

4 of Template 4 for bow centers

From the dark purple, cut:
8 of Template 2 for bow ends

4 of Template 4 for bow centers

From the dark blue, cut:
- 8 of Template 2 for bow ends
- 4 of Template 4 for bow centers

Assembling the Ohio Star Blocks

1. Sew the small triangles (B) together following the piecing diagram below. Press all seams toward the right triangle and sort the completed triangle pairs by color combination.

White Units

Make 12.

Make 12.

Make 12.

Make 12.

Multicolored Units

Make 4.

Make 4.

Make 4.

Make 4.

Make 4.

Make 4.

Make 4.

Make 4.

Make 4.

Make 4.

Make 4.

Make 4.

2. To complete the star-point squares, start with the white-blue units and select the 3 sets of multicolored units that have blue triangles on the right-hand side. Matching the center seams, sew a white-blue unit to a blue-multicolored unit to make 12 star-point squares. Each square should have 2 blue triangles, a white triangle on one side,

and either a pink, purple, or green triangle for the inside color.

Matching star points — Inside color

Make 12.

3. Repeat step 2 with the remaining sets of white units and the corresponding sets of multicolored units as shown below.

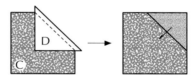

Make 12. Make 12. Make 12.

4. Sew a multicolor triangle (D) to the cut-off corner of floral (C) to make a corner square.

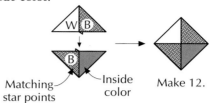

Make 48.

5. Assemble 4 matching star-point squares (B), 4 corner squares (CD), and 1 square (A) following the piecing diagram to complete an Ohio Star block. Follow the pressing arrows to ease assembly.

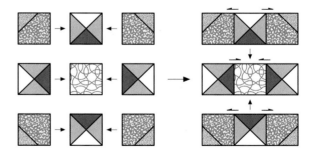

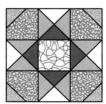

Make 12.

Assembling the Appliqué Blocks

1. Sew a 3" x 42" pink strip to each side of a 7½" x 42" white strip to make a strip unit as shown. Cut the strip units into a total of 24 segments, each 3" wide. Sew 2 segments to opposite sides of a 7½" x 12½" white rectangle to make an appliqué block.

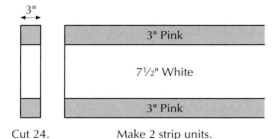

Cut 24.   Make 2 strip units.

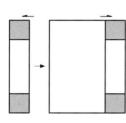

Make 12.

2. Refer to the Balloon and Bows placement guide on page 43 to position the appliqué pieces on the appliqué blocks. In the sample, the strings on the balloons are made from 6" lengths of ¼"-wide washable satin ribbon. Tuck the ribbon pieces under the balloons and bows before stitching so that the appliqué stitching holds them in place when completed. (If you prefer, embroider the strings instead.) Stitch appliqués in place and press the completed blocks.

Assembling and Finishing the Quilt

1. Arrange the Ohio Star blocks and the appliqué blocks in horizontal rows, alternating the blocks as shown in the quilt plan on page 39.

2. Sew the blocks together in horizontal rows. Press the seams toward the Ohio Star blocks. Join the rows, making sure to match the seams between the blocks.

3. Pin a white triangle to the center of the outside-edge appliqué blocks as shown. The base of the triangles will be stitched in place when the border

is attached; the loose edges will be appliquéd after the border is added.

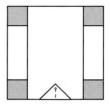

4. Add the 4½"-wide floral inner border, referring to "Straight-Cut Borders" on page 13. Repeat with the 4½"-wide balloon-print outer border.

5. Appliqué loose triangle edges to the inner border.

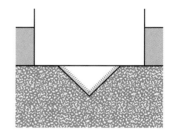

6. Layer the quilt top, batting, and backing; baste.

7. Quilt as desired, or follow the quilting suggestion below. Bind the edges.

8. Sign your quilt.

Quilting Suggestion

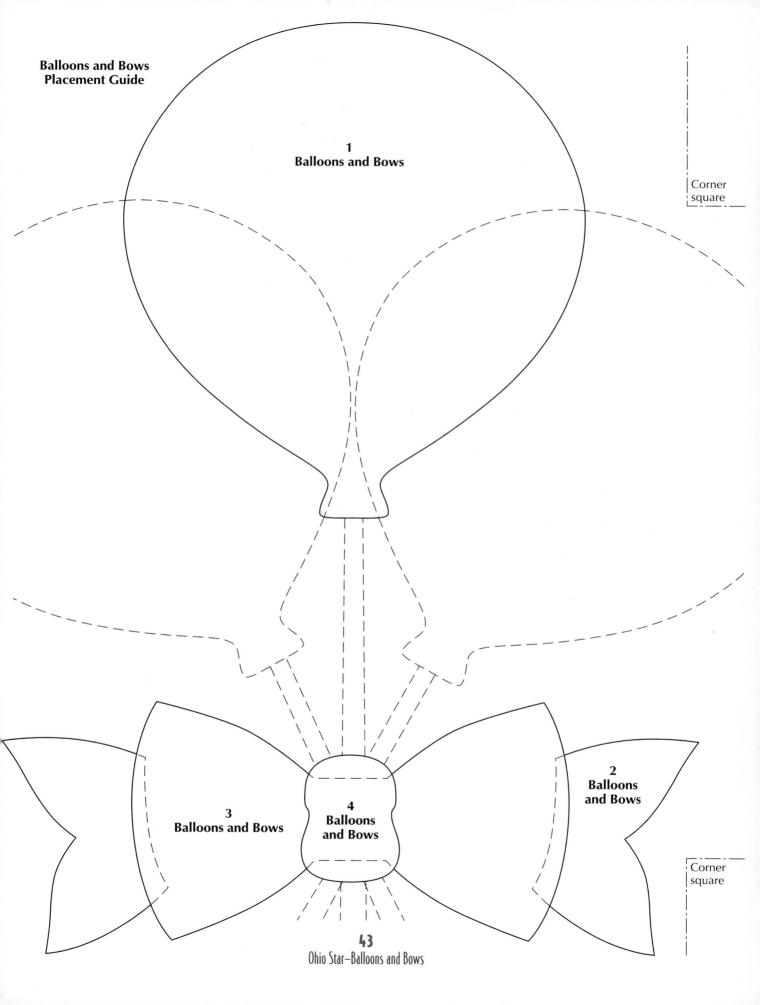

**Balloons and Bows
Placement Guide**

Corner
square

**1
Balloons and Bows**

**3
Balloons and Bows**

**4
Balloons
and Bows**

**2
Balloons
and Bows**

Corner
square

43
Ohio Star–Balloons and Bows

Churn Dash—Bunnykins

Finished Quilt Size: 44" x 56" • Finished Block Size: 12" • Color photo on page 70.

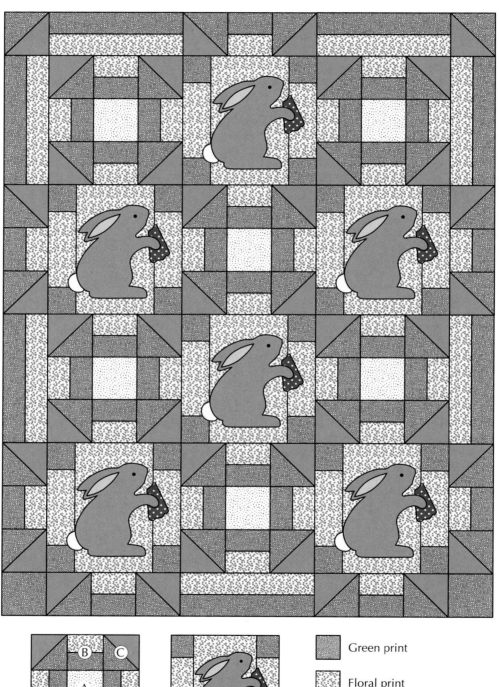

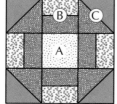

Churn Dash
Make 6.

Bunnykins
Make 6.

 Green print

 Floral print

Pink solid

 Yellow print

Materials: 44"-wide fabric

1¾ yds.	green print for pieced and appliqué blocks and pieced border
1⅝ yds.	floral print for pieced and appliqué blocks and pieced border
1 yd.	pink solid for pieced blocks, border, and bunnies
¼ yd.	yellow print for pieced blocks
Scrap	of light pink solid for inner ears
Scrap	of dark green print for lettuce leaves
Scrap	of white flannel for tails
3½ yds.	for backing
6	buttons, ⅜" diameter, for eyes (optional)

Cutting

Cut all strips across the width of the fabric.

From the green print, cut:

6 strips, each 2½" x 42", for pieced blocks (B) and pieced border
1 piece, 22" x 28", for half-square triangle units (C)
2 strips, each 3" x 42", for appliqué blocks
2 squares, each 4½" x 4½", for pieced border
5 strips, each 2½" x 42", for binding

From the floral print, cut:

6 strips, each 2½" x 42", for pieced blocks (B) and pieced border
1 strip, 7½" x 42", for appliqué blocks
2 strips, each 12½" x 42"
• crosscut into 6 rectangles, each 7½" x 12½", for appliqué blocks

From the pink solid, cut:

1 piece, 22" x 28", for half-square triangle units (C)
6 of Template 3 for bunnies

From the yellow print, cut:

1 strip, 4½" x 42"
• crosscut into 6 squares, each 4½" x 4½", for pieced blocks (A)

From the light pink solid, cut:

6 of Template 4 for inner ears

From the dark green print, cut:

6 of Template 2 for lettuce leaves

From the white flannel, cut:

6 of Template 1 for tail

Assembling the Churn Dash Blocks

1. Sew a 2½"-wide floral strip to a 2½"-wide green strip to make a strip unit as shown. Cut 3 strip units into 7 segments, each 12½" wide; set aside for the pieced border. Cut the remaining strip units into a total of 31 segments (B), each 4½" wide. Use 24 segments for the pieced blocks and 7 for the pieced border.

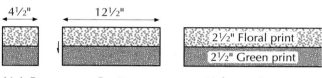

Unit B
Cut 31.   Cut 7.   Make 6 strip units.

2. Refer to "Making Half-Square Triangle Units" on page 8. Using the 22" x 28" pieces of pink and medium green, mark a grid of 4⅞" squares, 5 across and 4 down. Make a total of 40 half-square triangle units (C), 24 for the pieced blocks and 16 for the pieced borders. Press the seams toward the green triangles.

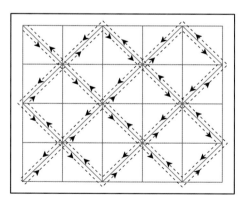

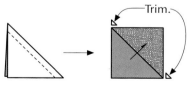

Unit C
Make 40.

3. Assemble the units following the piecing diagram to make a Churn Dash block. Reserve the remaining B and C units for the pieced border.

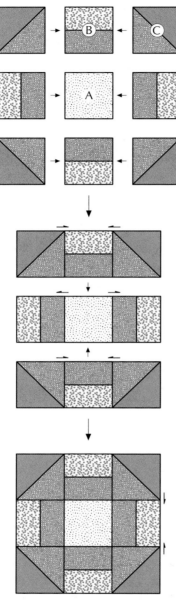

Make 6.

Assembling the Appliqué Blocks

1. Sew a 3" x 42" green strip to each side of a 7½" x 42" floral strip to make a strip unit as shown. Cut the strip unit into 12 segments, each 3" wide. Sew 2 segments to opposite sides of a 7½" x 12½" floral rectangle to make an appliqué block.

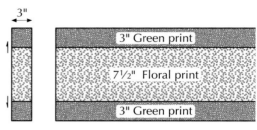

Cut 12.　　　　Make 1 strip unit.

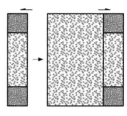

Make 6.

2. Refer to the Bunnykins placement guide on page 48 to position the appliqué pieces on the appliqué blocks. Stitch in place and press the completed blocks. Embroider the bunny eyes now if you are not using buttons.

Assembling and Finishing the Quilt

1. Arrange the Churn Dash blocks and appliqué blocks in horizontal rows, alternating the blocks as shown in the quilt plan on page 44.
2. Sew the blocks together in horizontal rows, pressing the seams toward the Churn Dash blocks. Join the rows, making sure to match the seams between the blocks.
3. Sew 2 C units to opposite sides of a B unit.

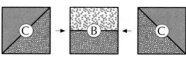

Make 7.

4. To make the pieced border, assemble the units made in the previous step and the 12½"-wide pieced segments as shown. Add the 2 remaining half-square triangle units (C) to each end of the top border strip. Add a 4½"-wide medium green square to each end of the bottom border strip.

Right Border

Left Border

Top Border

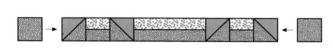

Bottom Border

5. Sew the left and right borders to the quilt top, then add the top and bottom borders. Be sure to orient the borders as shown in the quilt plan. Press the seams toward the pieced border.

6. Layer the quilt top, batting, and backing; baste.
7. Quilt as desired, or follow the quilting suggestion at right. Bind the edges.
8. Add buttons for eyes if you did not embroider them.
9. Sign your quilt.

Quilting Suggestion

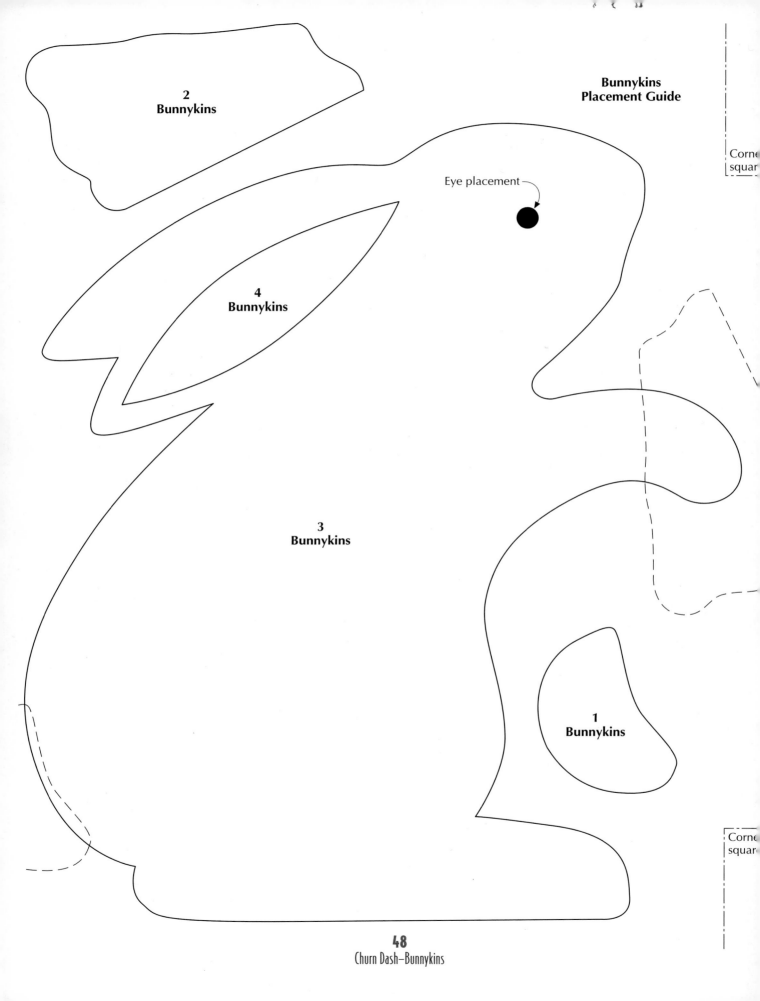

**2
Bunnykins**

Corne
squar

Eye placement

**4
Bunnykins**

**3
Bunnykins**

**1
Bunnykins**

Corne
squar

Sister's Choice—Tulip Medallion

Finished Quilt Size: 102" x 102" ▪ Finished Block Size: 12" ▪ Color photo on page 71.

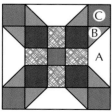

Sister's Choice
Make 25.

Tulip Medallion
Make 24.

■ Green print   ■ Rose solid

□ Cream print   ■ Burgundy solid

▨ Floral print

Materials: 44"-wide fabric

3¾ yds. green print for pieced blocks, pieced inner border, outer border, and appliqués

4⅛ yds. cream print for pieced and appliqué blocks

3 yds. floral print for pieced and appliqué blocks, pieced inner border, and binding

2⅝ yds. rose solid for pieced blocks, pieced inner border, middle border, and appliqués

1 yd. burgundy solid for pieced blocks and appliqués

9 yds. for backing

Cutting

Cut all strips across the width of the fabric.

From the green print, cut:

9 strips, each 3" x 42"
- crosscut into 126 squares, each 3" x 3", for blocks (C). Cut an additional 2 squares, each 3" x 3", from leftovers for a total of 128. Use 100 for pieced blocks and 28 for pieced inner border.

2 strips, each 2½" x 42", for pieced blocks

10 strips, each 4½" x 42", for outer border

96 of Template 2 for leaves

From the cream print, cut:

4 strips, each 7½" x 42", for appliqué blocks

5 strips, each 12½" x 42"
- crosscut into 25 rectangles, each 7½" x 12½", for appliqué blocks

16 strips, each 3" x 42", for pieced blocks (A)

From the floral print, cut:

4 strips, each 2½" x 42", for pieced blocks

12 strips, each 3" x 42", for pieced and appliqué blocks

2 strips, each 12½" x 42"
- crosscut into 16 strips, each 3" x 12½", for pieced inner border

10 strips, each 2½" x 42", for binding

From the rose solid, cut:

10 strips, each 3⅜" x 42"
- crosscut into 112 squares, each 3⅜" x 3⅜". Cut the squares once diagonally to yield 224 triangles. Use 200 for pieced blocks (B) and 24 for the pieced border.

10 strips, each 3" x 42", for middle border

96 of Template 3 for tulips

From the burgundy solid, cut:

8 strips, each 3" x 42", for pieced blocks

96 of Template 1 for tulip centers

Assembling the Sister's Choice Blocks

1. Sew a 3" x 42" floral strip to each side of a 2½" x 42" green print strip to make a strip unit as shown. Cut the strip units into a total of 25 segments, each 2½" wide.

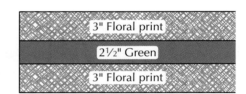

Cut 25.   Make 2 strip units.

2. Sew a 3" x 42" burgundy strip to each side of a 2½" x 42" floral strip to make a strip unit as shown. Cut the strip units into a total of 50 segments, each 3" wide.

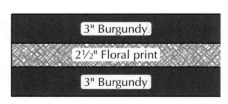

Cut 50.   Make 4 strip units.

3. Sew the segments from steps 1 and 2 together to make a nine-patch unit.

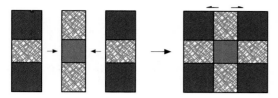

Make 25.

4. Make a plastic template of Template A on page 38. Place the template at one end of a 3"-wide cream strip. Use a pencil to mark the sides of the template and cut with scissors, or align a ruler with the edge of the template and cut along the edge of the ruler with your rotary cutter. Rotate the template along the strip as you cut the pieces. You should be able to cut 7 of piece A from each 42"-long strip.

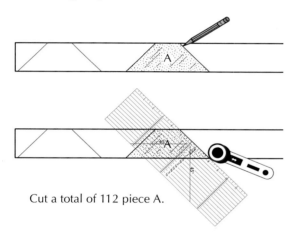

Cut a total of 112 piece A.

5. Sew 2 rose triangles (B) to the short sides of a cream piece A. Trim the dog ears.

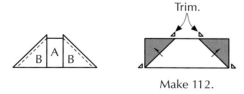

Make 112.

6. Sew an AB unit to the top and bottom of a nine-patch unit to make the center segment.

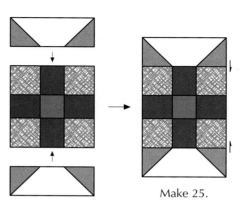

Make 25.

7. Sew a 3" green square (C) to each end of the remaining AB units. Sew these to the sides of a center segment to complete a Sister's Choice block. Set aside the remaining 12 ABC units for the pieced inner borders.

Make 62.

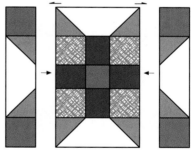

Make 25.

Assembling the Appliqué Block

1. Sew a 3" x 42" floral strip to each side of a 7½" x 42" cream strip to make a strip unit as shown. Cut the strip units into a total of 48 segments, each 3" wide. Sew 2 segments to opposite sides of a 7½" x 12½" white rectangle to make an appliqué block.

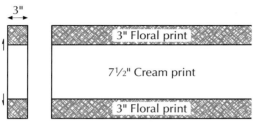

3"

3" Floral print

7½" Cream print

3" Floral print

Cut 48.　　　　Make 4 strip units.

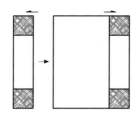

Make 24.

2. Refer to the Tulip Medallion placement guide on page 53 to position the appliqué pieces on the appliqué blocks. Stitch in place and press the completed blocks.

Assembling and Finishing the Quilt

1. Arrange the Sister's Choice blocks and appliqué blocks in horizontal rows, alternating the blocks as shown in the quilt plan on page 49.

2. Sew the blocks together in horizontal rows, pressing the seams toward the Sister's Choice blocks. Join the rows, making sure to match the seams between the blocks.

3. Sew the remaining ABC units and 3" x 12½" floral strips together as shown to make the pieced border.

4. Sew 2 pieced border strips to opposite sides of the quilt top. Add a 3" green square to each end of the remaining pieced border strips. Add these to the top and bottom edges. Press the seams toward the pieced border.

5. Add the 3"-wide rose middle border, referring to "Straight-Cut Borders" on page 13. Repeat with the 4½"-wide green outer border.

6. Layer the quilt top, batting, and backing; baste.

7. Quilt as desired, or follow the quilting suggestion below. Bind the edges.

8. Sign your quilt.

Quilting Suggestion

Pieced Border
Make 4.

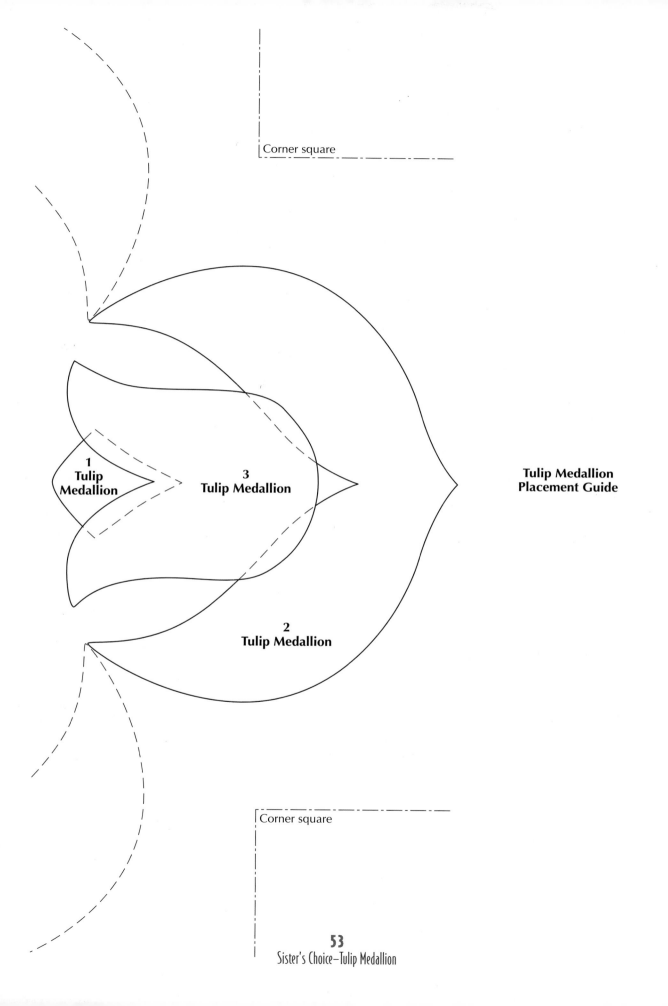

Corner square

1
Tulip
Medallion

3
Tulip Medallion

Tulip Medallion
Placement Guide

2
Tulip Medallion

Corner square

Wild Geese–Autumn Breeze

Finished Quilt Size: 74" x 74" • Finished Block Size: 12" • Color photo on page 72.

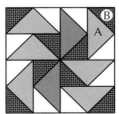

Wild Geese
Make 13.

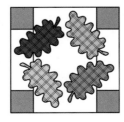

Autumn Breeze
Make 12.

Red plaid

Gold prints

Tan solid

Homespun plaids

Copper solid

54

Materials: 44"-wide fabric

3½ yds. red plaid for pieced blocks, pieced border, outer border, and binding
2½ yds. tan solid for pieced and appliqué blocks and pieced border
1⅛ yd. copper solid for pieced and appliqué blocks
½ yd. each of 3 different gold prints for pieced blocks
8 different fat quarters (18" x 22") of homespun plaids for oak leaves
4½ yds. for backing

Cutting

Cut all strips across the width of the fabric.

From the red plaid, cut:

11 strips, each 3⅞" x 42",
- crosscut into 72 squares, each 3⅞" x 3⅞". Cut the squares once diagonally to yield 144 triangles, 128 for pieced blocks (B) and 16 for pieced border.
2 strips, each 3½" x 42"
- crosscut into 20 squares, each 3½" x 3½", for pieced border
1 strip, 6½" x 42", for pieced border
8 strips, each 4½" x 42", for outer border
8 strips, each 2½" x 42", for binding

From the tan solid, cut:

3 strips, each 12½" x 42"
- crosscut into 12 rectangles, each 7½" x 12½", for appliqué blocks
2 strips, each 7½" x 42", for appliqué blocks
5 strips, each 3⅞" x 42"
- crosscut into 48 squares, each 3⅞" x 3⅞". Cut the squares once diagonally to yield 96 triangles; 80 for pieced blocks (B) and 16 for pieced border.

From the copper solid, cut:

4 strips, each 3" x 42", for appliqué blocks
2 strips, each 3½" x 42", for pieced border
7 squares, each 7¼" x 7¼"
- cut the squares twice diagonally to yield 28 triangles for pieced blocks (A). You will use only 26.

From each of the 3 gold prints, cut:

6 squares, each 7¼" x 7¼"
- cut 2 more squares for a total of 20. Cut the squares twice diagonally to yield 80 triangles for pieced blocks (A). You will use only 78.

From each of the 8 homespun fat quarters, cut:

6 of Template 1 (48 total)

Assembling the Wild Geese Blocks

1. Sew a small triangle (B) to each short side of a large triangle (A); trim the dog ears.

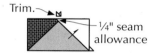

Trim.   ¼" seam allowance

Refer to the piecing diagrams for placement of the red plaid and tan piece triangles (B) to make geese units in the following color combinations.

Make 6 of each gold.
Make 6 copper.
(Make 24 total.)

Make 10 of each gold.
Make 16 copper.
(Make 46 total.)

Make 10 of each gold.
Make 4 copper.
(Make 34 total.)

2. Sort the geese units by unit number and color. For each block, use 6 assorted gold geese units and 2 copper geese units for a total of 8 geese units. Arrange the colors randomly within the block for an interesting mix of color and pattern. Sew the geese units together in pairs. Sew the pairs together in rows; then join the rows to complete the block. Follow the piecing diagrams to make the following block combinations. Press the seams as indicated in the diagrams to ease block assembly.

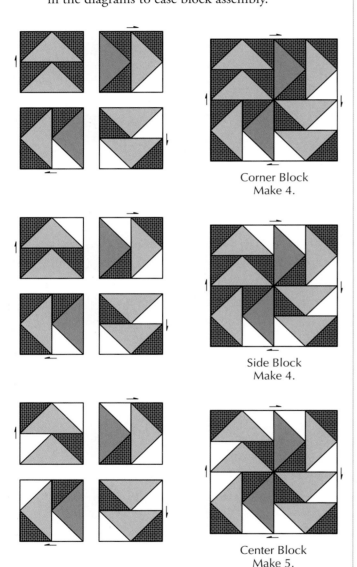

Corner Block
Make 4.

Side Block
Make 4.

Center Block
Make 5.

Assembling the Appliqué Blocks

1. Sew a 3" x 42" copper strip to each side of a 7½" x 42" tan strip to make a strip unit as shown. Cut the strip units into a total of 24 segments, each 3" wide. Sew 2 segments to opposite sides of a 7½" x 12½" tan rectangle to make an appliqué block.

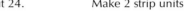
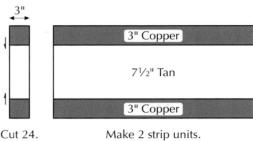

Cut 24.   Make 2 strip units.

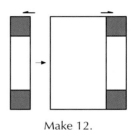

Make 12.

2. Refer to the Autumn Breeze placement guide on page 58 to position appliqué pieces on the appliqué blocks. Mix the leaf fabrics within each block for a random look. Stitch in place and press the completed blocks.

Assembling and Finishing the Quilt

1. Arrange the corner, side, and center Flying Geese blocks and the appliqué blocks as shown in the quilt plan on page 54.
2. Sew the blocks together in horizontal rows, pressing the seams toward the Flying Geese blocks. Join the rows, making sure to match the seams between the blocks.
3. For pieced border, sew a tan triangle (B) to a red plaid triangle (B).

Make 16.

4. Sew 2 tan-red half-square triangle units together as shown. Add a 3½" red square to each end.

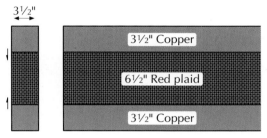

Make 8.

5. Sew a 3½" x 42" copper strip to each long side of a 6½" x 42" red plaid strip to make a strip unit. Cut the strip unit into 12 segments, each 3½" wide.

3½"

3½" Copper
6½" Red plaid
3½" Copper

Cut 12.   Make 1 strip units.

6. Sew the border segments together to make the pieced border strips.

Pieced Borders
Make 4.

7. Sew 2 pieced border strips to opposite sides of the quilt top, matching the seams between the pieces. Rotate the pieced border strips so that the tan triangles face toward the center of the quilt as shown in the quilt plan. Press seams toward the pieced border.

8. Sew a 3½" red plaid square to each end of the remaining pieced border strips. Sew these to the top and bottom edges of the quilt top, matching the seams between the pieces. Press the seams toward the pieced border.

9. Add the 4½"-wide red plaid border, referring to "Straight-Cut Borders" on page 13.

10. Layer the quilt top, batting, and backing; baste.

11. Quilt as desired, or follow the quilting suggestion above right. Bind the edges.

12. Sign your quilt.

Quilting Suggestion

Center
of block

Autumn Breeze

Corner square

**Autumn Breeze
Placement Guide**

Pine Burr–Jack Frost

Finished Quilt Size: 97" x 97" • Finished Block Size: 12" • Color photo on page 73.

Pine Burr
Make 25.

Jack Frost
Make 24.

59

Materials: 44"-wide fabric

7¼ yds. blue print for pieced and appliqué blocks, pieced border, outer border, and binding

5¼ yds. white print for pieced and appliqué blocks and appliqués

8½ yds. for backing

Cutting

Cut all strips across the width of the fabric.

From the blue print, cut:

5 strips, each 3⅜" x 42"
- crosscut into 50 squares, each 3⅜" x 3 ⅜". Cut the squares once diagonally to yield 100 triangles for pieced blocks (B).

2 strips, each 24" x 42"
- cut the strips in half to yield 4 pieces, each 21" x 24", for making half-square triangles (D)

8 strips, each 2½" x 42"
- crosscut into 112 rectangles, each 3" x 2½", for pieced blocks (E) and pieced border

5 strips, each 7½" x 42", for appliqué blocks and pieced border

5 strips, each 12½" x 42"
- crosscut into 24 rectangles, each 7½" x 12½", for appliqué blocks

10 strips, each 4½" x 42", for outer border

10 strips, each 2½" x 42", for binding

From the white print, cut:

3 strips, each 4" x 42"
- crosscut into 25 squares, each 4" x 4", for pieced blocks (A)

6 strips, each 4⅜" x 42"
- crosscut into 50 squares, each 4⅜" x 4⅜". Cut the squares once diagonally to yield 100 triangles for pieced blocks (C).

2 strips, each 24" x 42"
- cut the strips in half to yield 4 pieces, each 21" x 24", for making half-square triangles (D)

10 strips, each 3" x 42", for appliqué blocks and pieced border

6 strips, each 10½" x 42"
- crosscut into 24 squares, each 10½" x 10½", for snowflake appliqués

Assembling the Pine Burr Blocks

1. Sew 2 small blue triangles (B) to opposite sides of a 4" white square (A), then sew 2 blue triangles to the remaining sides.

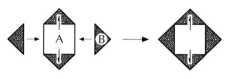

Make 25.

2. Sew 2 large white triangles (C) to opposite sides of the AB square, then sew 2 white triangles to the remaining sides.

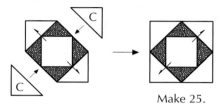

Make 25.

3. Refer to "Making Half-Square Triangle Units" on page 8. Using the 21" x 24" pieces of white and blue fabric, mark a grid of 2⅞" squares, 8 across and 6 down. Make a total of 352 half-square triangle units (D). Press the seams toward the blue triangles.

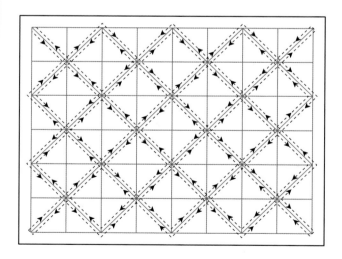

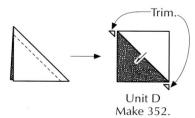

Unit D
Make 352.

4. Sew the half-square triangle units (D) into pairs to make 2 different DD units.

Make 31.   Make 31.

5. Sew one of each type of DD unit to opposite sides of a blue rectangle (E).

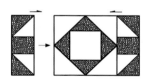

Make 62.

6. Sew 2 half-square triangle units (D) to opposite sides of a blue rectangle (E).

Make 50.

7. Sew 2 units made in step 6 to opposite sides of a center square (ABC) to make the center segment.

8. Sew 2 units made in step 5 to the top and bottom of the center segment to complete the Pine Burr block. Reserve remaining units for pieced border.

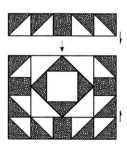

Make 25.

Assembling the Appliqué Blocks

1. Sew a 3" x 42" white strip to each side of a 7½" x 42" blue strip to make a strip unit as shown. Cut the strip units into a total of 64 segments, each 3" wide. Sew 2 segments to opposite sides of a 7½" x 12½" blue rectangle to make an appliqué block. Reserve remaining segments for pieced border.

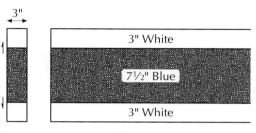

3"

3" White

7½" Blue

3" White

Cut 64.   Make 5 strip units.

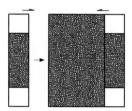

Make 24.

2. Fold the 10½" squares in half, then in quarters, and press. Make a paper or plastic template of the snowflake pattern on page 63. Place the straight sides of the snowflake template on the folded edges of the fabric as shown and trace around the snowflake. Pin the layers together and cut out the snowflake through all 4 layers of folded fabric at the same time. This is the same method you used to make paper snowflakes as a child.

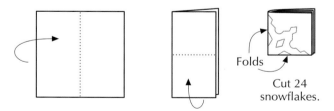

Folds

Cut 24 snowflakes.

3. Refer to the Jack Frost placement guide on page 63 to position the snowflakes on the appliqué blocks. Stitch the snowflakes in place and press the completed blocks.

Assembling and Finishing the Quilt

1. Arrange the Pine Burr blocks and appliqué blocks in horizontal rows, alternating the blocks as shown in the quilt plan on page 59.
2. Sew the blocks together in horizontal rows, pressing the seams toward the Pine Burr blocks. Join the rows, making sure to match the seams between the blocks.
3. Sew the remaining units together as shown to make the pieced border strips.

Make 4.

4. Sew 2 pieced border strips to opposite sides of the quilt top. Sew a half-square triangle unit (D) to each end of the remaining pieced border strips, rotating the units as shown. Sew the borders to the top and bottom edges. Press the seams toward the border.

Top and Bottom Borders

5. Add the 4½"-wide blue outer border, referring to "Straight-Cut Borders" on page 13.
6. Layer the quilt top, batting, and backing; baste.
7. Quilt as desired, or follow the quilting suggestion below. Bind the edges.
8. Sign your quilt.

Quilting Suggestion

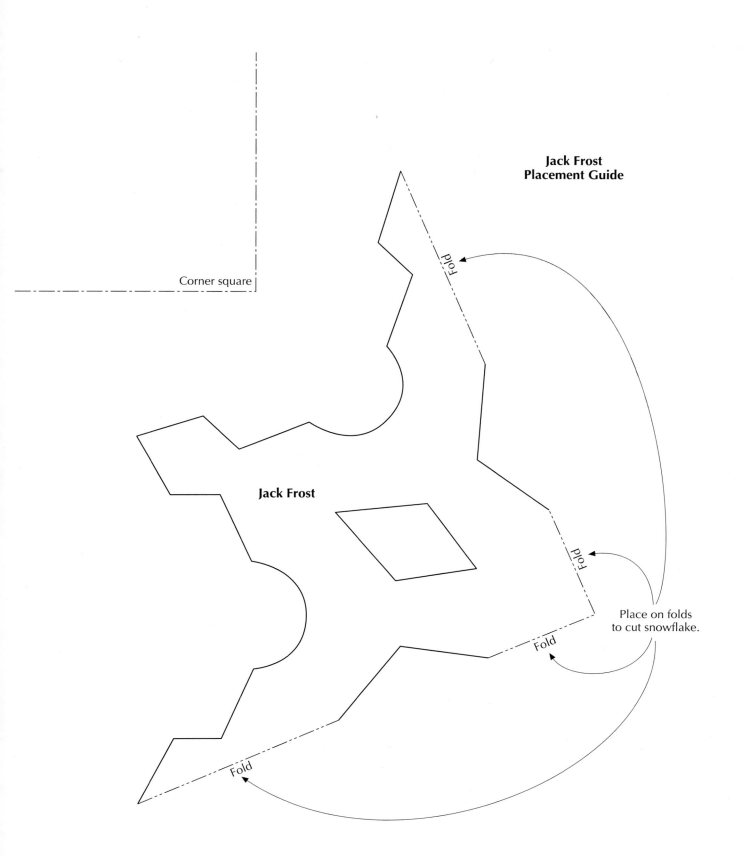

Corner square

**Jack Frost
Placement Guide**

Fold

Fold

Jack Frost

Fold

Place on folds
to cut snowflake.

Fold

Ohio Star–Ring-a-Rosy

Finished Quilt Size: 84" x 108" • Finished Block Size: 12" • Color photo on page 74.

Ohio Star
Make 24.

Ring-a-Rosy
Make 17.

Black solid

Green solid

Amish colors
(7 different solids)

Materials: 44"-wide fabric

7¾ yds. black solid for pieced and appliqué blocks, borders, and binding
1¼ yds. green solid for pieced blocks and leaves
⅞ yd. each of 7 Amish colors for pieced blocks and appliqués
6 yds. for backing

Cutting

Cut all strips across the width of the fabric.

From the black solid, cut:

11 strips, each 4½" x 42"
- crosscut into 96 squares, each 4½" x 4½". Use Cut-off Template A on page 68 to remove one corner from each square (C).

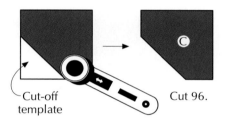

Cut-off template   Cut 96.

6 strips, each 5¼" x 42"
- crosscut into 48 squares, each 5¼" x 5¼". Cut squares twice diagonally to yield 192 quarter-square triangles (B).

4 strips, each 7½" x 28", for appliqué blocks
4 strips, each 12½" x 42"
- crosscut into 17 rectangles, each 7½" x 12½", for appliqué blocks

4 strips, each 12½" x 36½", for side borders
3 strips, each 12½" x 42"
- cut 1 strip in half and sew a half-strip to 1 end of the remaining 2 strips for top and bottom borders

10 strips, each 2½" x 42", for binding
68 of Template 3 for flower centers

From the green solid, cut:

3 squares, each 4½" x 4½", for pieced blocks (A)
1 strip, 3" x 28", for appliqué blocks
1 strip, 5¼" x 42"
- crosscut each strip into 6 squares, each 5¼" x 5¼". Cut the squares twice diagonally to yield 24 triangles for pieced blocks (B).

1 strip, 3⅜" x 42"
- crosscut into 6 squares, each 3⅜" x 3⅜". Cut the squares once diagonally to yield 12 triangles for pieced blocks (D).

4 of Template 2 for flowers
136 of Template 1 for leaves

From *each* of the 7 Amish colors, cut:

3 squares, each 4½" x 4½", (21 total) for pieced blocks (A)
1 strip, 3" x 28", for appliqué blocks
1 strip, 5¼" x 42"
- crosscut each strip into 6 squares, each 5¼" x 5¼". Cut the squares twice diagonally to yield 24 triangles of each color for pieced blocks (B).

1 strip, 3⅜" x 42"
- crosscut into 6 squares, each 3⅜" x 3⅜". Cut the squares once diagonally to yield 12 triangles of each color for pieced blocks (D).

From Template 2
- cut 8 each of 7 colors plus 4 additional Template 2 from 3 colors for a total of 68 flowers. You need 4 matching flowers for each appliqué block.

Assembling the Ohio Star Blocks

1. Sew an Amish-color triangle (B) to a black triangle (B) as shown. Sort the pairs by color.

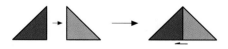

2. Sew pairs of B triangles together to make the star-point squares, matching the Amish colors within the units.

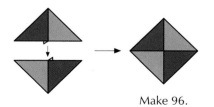

Make 96.

3. Sew a triangle (D) to the cut-off corner of black (C) to make a corner square.

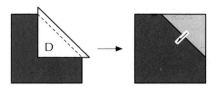

Make 96.

4. To complete an Ohio Star block, assemble 4 matching star-point squares (B), 4 corner squares (CD), and 1 square (A) following the piecing diagram below.

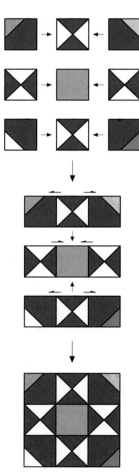

Make 24.

Assembling the Appliqué Blocks

1. Sew a different color 3" x 28" Amish strip to each long side of a 7½" x 28" black strip to make a strip unit as shown. Cut the strip units into a total of 34 segments, each 3"-wide. Sew 2 segments to opposite sides of a 7½" x 12½" black rectangle to make an appliqué block.

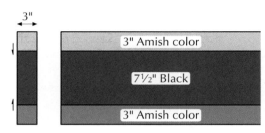

3"

3" Amish color

7½" Black

3" Amish color

Cut 34.   Make 4 strip units 28" long.

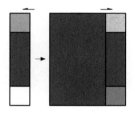

Make 17.

3. Refer to the Ring-a-Rosy placement guide on page 68 to position the appliqué pieces on the appliqué blocks. Stitch in place and press the completed blocks.

Assembling and Finishing the Quilt

1. Arrange the Ohio Star blocks and the appliqué blocks in horizontal rows, alternating the blocks as shown in the quilt plan on page 64. Reserve 6 Ohio Star blocks for the border.

2. Sew the blocks together in horizontal rows, pressing the seams toward the Ohio Star blocks. Join the rows, making sure to match the seams between the blocks.

3. Trim the top and bottom border strips to 60½" and stitch them to the top and bottom edges of the quilt. Press the seams toward the borders.

4. Sew the remaining Ohio Star blocks to the black 12½" x 36½" strips; press the seams toward the black. Sew these to the sides of the quilt top, matching seams where the borders intersect.

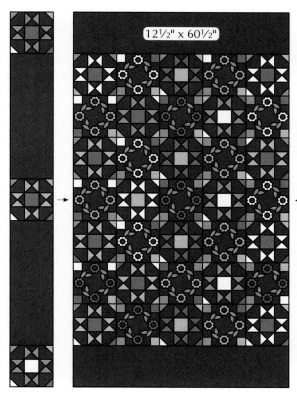

12½" x 60½"

12½" x 36½"

12½" x 36½"

5. Layer the quilt top, batting, and backing; baste.
6. Quilt as desired, or follow the quilting suggestion below. Bind the edges.
7. Sign your quilt.

Quilting Suggestion

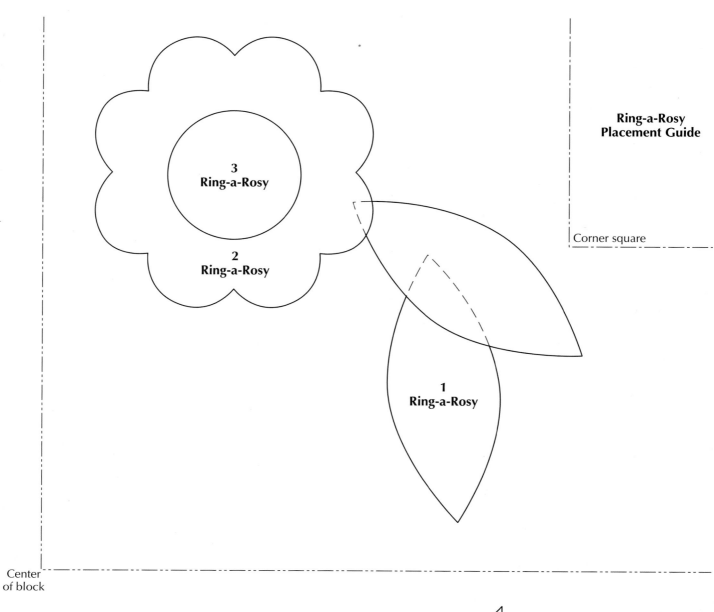

**Ring-a-Rosy
Placement Guide**

Corner square

3
Ring-a-Rosy

2
Ring-a-Rosy

1
Ring-a-Rosy

Center
of block

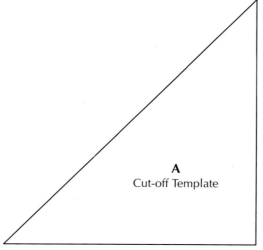

A
Cut-off Template

QUILT GALLERY

Ohio Star—Balloons and Bows by Deborah J. Moffett-Hall, January 1995, Hatfield, Pennsylvania, 64" x 88". This quilt is the hands-down favorite among my daughter Michelle's friends. One of them declared, "It looks like a birthday party for your bed!" Directions begin on page 39.

Churn Dash—Bunnykins, pieced by Beth G. Hertz, appliquéd and quilted by Deborah J. Moffett-Hall, February 1995, Hatfield, Pennsylvania, 44" x 56". This pattern was designed for Beth's four-year-old daughter, Janet, who loves bunnies. Directions begin on page 44.

Sister's Choice—Tulip Medallion by Deborah J. Moffett-Hall, February 1995, Hatfield, Pennsylvania, 102" x 102". It's fun to decorate according to the seasons, and this quilt is terrific for spring and summer. Changing the quilt changes the room, and it's as easy as making the bed. Directions begin on page 49.

Wild Geese—Autumn Breeze by Deborah J. Moffett-Hall, September 1994, Hatfield, Pennsylvania, 74" x 74". Deep fall colors make this quilt warm and inviting. Light a fire in the grate and snuggle under the fall foliage with a friend to watch a classic film on television. Directions begin on page 54.

Pine Burr—Jack Frost by Deborah J. Moffett-Hall, January 1995, Hatfield, Pennsylvania, 97" x 97". White snowflakes on a blue background look crisp and cool, just like a midnight snowfall. Two-color quilts make graphic statements; block patterns are highly defined and lines are strong and clean. Directions begin on page 59.

Ohio Star—Ring-a-Rosy, pieced by Marla and Robert Moyer, East Greenville, Pennsylvania; appliquéd and quilted by Deborah J. Moffett-Hall, April 1995, Hatfield, Pennsylvania, 84" x 108". Marla and Bob are a team: Bob cuts the pieces and Marla stitches the quilts. Directions begin on page 64.

Shoofly—Dolphin Dance by Deborah J. Moffett-Hall, July 1995, Hatfield, Pennsylvania, 79" x 103". For our fifth wedding anniversary, my husband and I went on a cruise to Bermuda. Looking out our porthole, we were enchanted to see dolphins playing in the wake. The beautiful animals streaked under the surface until they reached the crest of the wake, then burst out of the water, landed on the wake, and rode it for a few moments before diving out of view. Directions begin on page 81.

Wild Geese—Holly Holly, pieced by Beth G. Hertz, appliquéd and quilted by Deborah J. Moffett-Hall, March 1994, Hatfield, Pennsylvania, 48" x 48". After piecing "Wild Geese—Autumn Breeze" (page 72), I wanted to see what other designs I could make with the Wild Geese block by changing the color placement. I like the way the pointed edges of the white areas mimic the serrated holly leaves. Directions begin on the opposite page.

Wild Geese–Holly Holly

Finished Quilt Size: 48" x 48" · Finished Block Size: 12" · Color photo opposite.

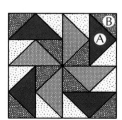

Wild Geese
Make 5.

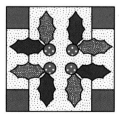

Holly Holly
Make 4.

Green print		Green solid
White print		Red paisley
Red solid		Red pindot

Materials: 44"-wide fabric

1¼ yds.   green print for pieced blocks, holly, pieced
           border, outer border, and binding
1⅛ yds.   white print for pieced and appliqué
           blocks and pieced border
  ¾ yd.   red solid for pieced and appliqué
           blocks, pieced border, and outer border
  ¾ yd.   green solid for pieced blocks and holly
  ⅝ yd.   red paisley for pieced blocks
  ⅛ yd.   or scrap of red pindot for holly berries
  3 yds.   for backing

Cutting

Cut all strips across the width of the fabric.

From the green print, cut:

2 strips, each 3⅞" x 42"
- crosscut into 20 squares, each 3⅞" x 3⅞". Cut
the squares once diagonally to yield 40 triangles
for pieced blocks (B).

4 strips, each 3½" x 42½". If your strips are not
42½" long, cut an extra strip (5 total) and piece
the outer border.

4 squares, each 3½" x 3½", for pieced border

5 strips, each 2½" x 42", for binding

16 of Template 1 for holly leaves

From the white print, cut:

3 strips, each 3⅞" x 42"
- crosscut into 24 squares, each 3⅞" x 3⅞". Cut
the squares once diagonally to yield 48 triangles,
40 for the blocks (B) and 8 for the pieced border.

1 strip, 7½" x 42", for appliqué blocks

1 strip, 12½" x 42"
- crosscut into 4 rectangles, each 7½" x 12½", for
appliqué blocks

From the red solid, cut:

1 strip, 3⅞" x 42"
- crosscut into 4 squares, each 3⅞" x 3⅞". Cut
the squares once diagonally to yield 8 triangles
for pieced border.

2 strips, each 3" x 42", for appliqué blocks

1 strip, 12½" x 42"
- crosscut into 12 segments, each 3½" x 12½". Set
aside 8 segments for the pieced border. Cut each of
the remaining segments into 3 squares, each 3½" x
3½", for a total of 12 squares for the borders.

From the green solid, cut:

2 strips, each 7¼" x 42"
- crosscut into 10 squares, each 7¼" x 7¼". Cut
the squares once diagonally to yield 20 triangles
for pieced blocks (A).

16 of Template 1 for holly leaves

From the red paisley, cut:

2 strips, each 7¼" x 42"
- crosscut into 10 squares, each 7¼" x 7¼". Cut
the squares once diagonally to yield 20 triangles
for pieced blocks (A).

From the red pindot, cut:

20 of Template 2 for berries

Assembling the Wild Geese Blocks

1. Referring to step 1 on page 55, sew a small white
triangle (B) and a small green-print triangle (B) to
each large green-solid triangle (A). Make 20 green
units. Sew a small white triangle (B) and a small
green-print triangle (B) to each large red paisley
triangle (A). Make 20 red units. Trim the dog ears.

 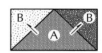

Green Unit
Make 20.

Red Unit
Make 20.

2. Sew a green unit on top of a red
unit to make a green/red unit.

Green/Red Unit
Make 20.

3. To make a Wild
Geese block, sew 4
green/red units to-
gether following the
piecing diagram.

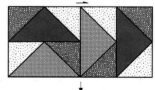

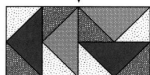

Make 5.

Assembling the Appliqué Blocks

1. Sew a 3"-wide red-solid strip to each side of a white 7½" x 42" strip to make a strip unit as shown. Cut the strip unit into 8 segments, each 3" wide. Sew 2 segments to opposite sides of a 7½" x 12½" white rectangle to make an appliqué block.

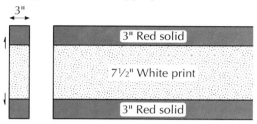

3"

3" Red solid

7½" White print

3" Red solid

Cut 8.   Make 1 strip unit.

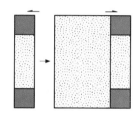

Make 4.

2. Refer to the Holly Holly placement guide on page 80 to position appliqué pieces on the appliqué blocks. Stitch in place and press the completed block.

Assembling and Finishing the Quilt

1. Arrange the Wild Geese blocks and appliqué blocks in horizontal rows, alternating the blocks as shown in the quilt plan on page 77.
2. Sew the blocks together in horizontal rows, pressing the seams toward the appliqué blocks. Join the rows, making sure to match the seams between blocks.
3. For the pieced border, sew a small red triangle (B) and a small white triangle (B) together to make a half-square triangle unit. Trim the dog ears.

B

B

Trim.

Make 8.

4. Join 2 red-white half-square triangle units. Add a 3½" red-solid square to each end as shown.

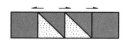

Make 4.

5. Sew a 3½" x 12½" red solid strip to each end of the unit made in step 4 to make a pieced border strip.

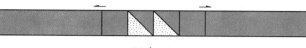

Make 4.

6. Sew 2 borders to opposite sides of the quilt top, matching the seams where they intersect. Be sure to orient the white triangles toward the center of the quilt as shown in the quilt plan. Press the seams toward the borders.
7. Sew a 3½" green square to each end of the remaining pieced border strips. Add these to the top and bottom edges of the quilt top. Press the seams toward the borders.
8. Measure the width and length of the quilt top (should be 42½"). If your outer-border strips are not 42½" long, join the strips to make 1 long strip and cut 4 strips to fit. Sew 2 border strips to opposite sides of the quilt top.
9. Sew a 3½" red solid square to each end of the remaining 3½"-wide green outer-border strips. Sew these to the top and bottom edges of the quilt top.
10. Layer the quilt top, batting, and backing; baste.
11. Quilt as desired, or follow the quilting suggestion below. Bind the edges.
12. Sign your quilt.

Quilting Suggestion

Center
of block

**2
Holly Holly**

**1
Holly Holly**

Corner square

**Holly Holly
Placement Guide**

Shoofly–Dolphin Dance

Finished Quilt Size: 79" x 103" • Finished Block Size: 12" • Color photo on page 75.

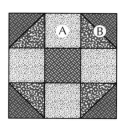

Shoofly
Make 18.

Dolphin Dance
Make 17.

Green print		Multicolor floral
Water print		Gray prints

Materials: 44"-wide fabric

3⅜ yds. green print for pieced blocks, outer border, and binding
3¼ yds. water print for pieced and appliqué blocks
2½ yds. multicolor floral for pieced and appliqué blocks, and inner border
⅞ yd. each of 3 different gray prints for dolphins
6⅛ yds. for backing
34 beads for eyes (optional)

Cutting

Cut all strips across the width of the fabric.

From the green print, cut:
2 strips, each 4½" x 42", for pieced blocks
1 piece, 27" x 42", for pieced blocks
  • cut into 2 pieces, 27" x 21" and 21" x 21"
9 strips, each 6" x 42", for outer border
9 strips, each 2½" x 42", for binding

From the water print, cut:
8 strips, each 4½" x 42", for pieced blocks
  • crosscut 4 strips into 36 squares, each 4½" x 4½"
3 strips, each 7½" x 42", for appliqué blocks
4 strips, each 12½" x 42"
  • crosscut into 17 rectangles, each 7½" x 12½", for appliqué blocks

From the multicolor floral, cut:
1 piece, 27" x 42", for pieced blocks
  • cut into 2 pieces, 27" x 21" and 21" x 21"
6 strips, each 3" x 42", for appliqué blocks
8 strips, each 4½" x 42", for inner border

From each of the 3 gray prints, cut:
11 of Template 1 for dolphins; cut 1 additional dolphin for a total of 34

Assembling the Shoofly Blocks

1. Refer to "Making Half-Square Triangle Units" on page 8. Using the 21" x 27" floral and green pieces, mark a grid of 4⅞" squares, 5 across and 4 down. Repeat with the 21" x 21" pieces of fabric,

marking a grid of 4⅞" squares, 4 across and 4 down. Make a total of 72 half-square triangle units. Press the seams toward the green triangles.

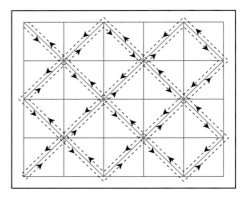

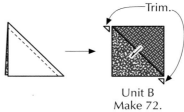

Unit B
Make 72.

2. Sew a 4½" x 42" water-print strip to each side of a 4½" x 42" green strip to make a strip unit as shown. Cut the strip units into a total of 18 segments, each 4½" wide.

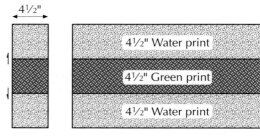

Cut 18.   Make 2 strip units.

3. Sew 2 half-square triangle units to opposite sides of a 4½" water-print square, keeping the floral triangle oriented toward the water-print square.

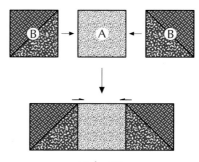

Make 36.

4. To complete the Shoofly block, assemble the segments from steps 2 and 3, following the piecing diagram below.

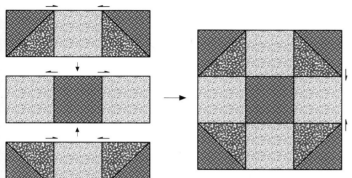

Make 18.

Assembling the Appliqué Blocks

1. Sew a 3" x 42" floral strip to each side of a 7½" x 42" water-print strip to make a strip unit as shown. Cut the strip units into a total of 34 segments, each 3" wide. Sew 2 segments to opposite sides of a 7½" x 12½" water-print rectangle to make an appliqué block.

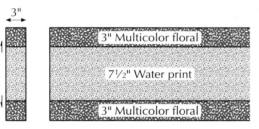

Cut 34.   Make 3 strip units.

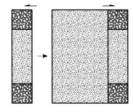

Make 17.

2. Refer to the Dolphin Dance placement guide on page 84 to position the appliqué pieces on the appliqué blocks. Stitch in place and press the completed block. Embroider the dolphin mouth line. You can also embroider the eyes if you are not using buttons.

Assembling and Finishing the Quilt

1. Arrange the Shoofly blocks and appliqué blocks in horizontal rows, alternating the blocks as shown in the quilt plan on page 81.

2. Sew the blocks together in horizontal rows, pressing the seams toward the Shoofly blocks. Join the rows, matching the seams between the blocks.

3. Add the 4½"-wide floral inner border, referring to "Straight-Cut Borders" on page 13. Repeat with the 6"-wide green outer border.

4. Layer the quilt top, batting, and backing; baste.

5. Quilt as desired, or follow the quilting suggestion below. Bind the edges.

6. Add buttons for eyes if you did not embroider them.

7. Sign your quilt.

Quilting Suggestion

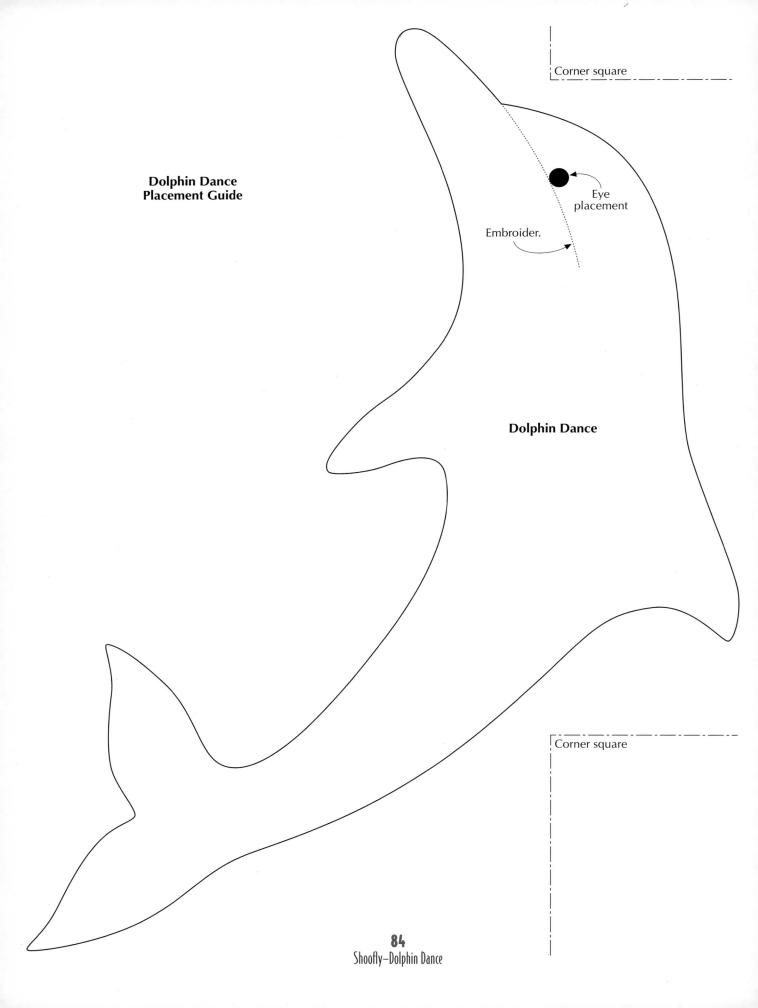

**Dolphin Dance
Placement Guide**

Corner square

Eye
placement

Embroider.

Dolphin Dance

Corner square

84
Shoofly–Dolphin Dance

YARDAGE CHARTS

Standard Mattress Sizes

	Width	Length
Crib	23"	46"
Twin	39"	75"
Full	54"	75"
Queen	60"	80"
King	78"	80"

Quilt Sizes and Layouts for 12" Blocks without Borders

	Size	Layout	Pieced Blocks	Appliqué Blocks
Wall/Baby	36" x 36"	3 x 3	5	4
Crib/Youth	36" x 48"	3 x 4	6	6
Twin	48" x 84"	4 x 7	14	14
Full	60" x 84"	5 x 7	18	17
Queen	84" x 84"	7 x 7	25	24
King	108" x 108"	9 x 9	41	40

Charts

Sometimes you find the perfect pattern for your next quilt, but the directions are for the wrong size. For instance, the quilt you like is a wall hanging, but you want to make a queen-size masterpiece. How much of each fabric do you need to make a larger quilt? I hear this question all the time, so I've included a handy chart that indicates the number of pieces and the yardage needed to make blocks for six quilt sizes. You can also use the charts to determine how much fabric you need to make a quilt smaller than a given pattern.

To use the charts, make a copy of the block pattern and assign a fabric or color to each piece; I find it helpful to use colored pencils. Refer to the chart to determine the number of pieces and the amount of fabric required for each piece. When the same fabric is assigned to two or more pattern pieces, add the measurements to determine the total yardage of any given color.

Either add the yardage measurement:
 ⅜ yard + ¼ yard (⅝ yard) = ⅝ yard
Or add the inches and divide by 36:
 10" + 14" + 30" = 54"
 54" divided by 36 = 1½ yards

Requirements in yards are rounded up to the nearest ⅛ or ⅓ yard. Be sure to buy extra fabric to allow for shrinkage.

The icons ◻ and ⊠ in the cutting charts indicate to cut the squares either once or twice diagonally for half-square or quarter-square triangles. (See page 7.)

▲▼▲▼▲▼▲▼▲▼▲▼▲▼▲▼**IMPORTANT NOTE**▼▲▼▲▼▲▼▲▼▲▼▲▼▲▼

These charts are for blocks only. You will need to determine the amount of fabric required for borders. Refer to "Adding Borders" on page 13 to see how to measure your quilt for borders. Cut all strips across the fabric width (42" width for crosswise grain).

▲▼▲▼▲▼▲▼▲▼▲▼▲▼▲▼▲▼▲▼▲▼▲▼▲▼▲▼▲▼▲▼▲

Appliqué Blocks

Piece	1st Cut Strip Width	2nd Cut Dimensions	No. of Pieces from 1 Strip
A	12½"	7½" x 12½"	5
B	7½"	3" x 7½"	14
C	3"	3" x 3"	14

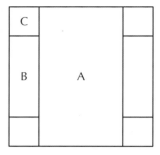

Appliqué Block

Quilt Size	No. of Blocks	Piece	No. of Pieces	No. of Strips to Cut	Yardage Required In Inches	In Yards
Wall	4	A	4	1	12½	⅜
		B	8	1	7½	¼
		C	16	2	6	¼
Crib	6	A	6	2	25	¾
		B	12	1	7½	¼
		C	24	2	6	¼
Twin	14	A	14	3	37½	1⅛
		B	28	2	15	½
		C	56	4	12	⅜
Full	17	A	17	4	50	1½
		B	34	3	22½	⅝
		C	68	5	15	½
Queen	24	A	24	5	62½	1¾
		B	48	4	30	⅞
		C	96	7	21	⅝
King	40	A	40	8	100	2⅞
		B	80	6	45	1¼
		C	160	12	36	1

Wild Geese

Piece	1st Cut Strip Width	2nd Cut Dimensions	No. of Pieces from 1 Strip	3rd Cut
A1	7¼"	7¼" x 7¼"	5	20 ⊠
A2	7¼"	7¼" x 7¼"	5	20 ⊠
B1	3⅞"	3⅞" x 3⅞"	10	20 ◻
B2	3⅞"	3⅞" x 3⅞"	10	20 ◻
B3	3⅞"	3⅞" x 3⅞"	10	20 ◻

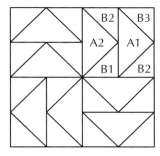

Wild Geese

Quilt Size	No. of Blocks	Piece	No. of Pieces	No. of Strips to Cut	Yardage Required In Inches	In Yards
Wall	5	A1	20	1	7¼	¼
		A2	20	1	7¼	¼
		B1	20	1	3⅞	⅛
		B2	40	2	7¾	¼
		B3	20	1	3⅞	⅛
Crib	6	A1	24	2	14½	½
		A2	24	2	14½	½
		B1	24	2	7¾	¼
		B2	48	3	11⅝	⅜
		B3	24	2	7¾	¼
Twin	14	A1	56	3	21¾	⅝
		A2	56	3	21¾	⅝
		B1	56	3	11⅝	⅜
		B2	112	6	23¼	¾
		B3	56	3	11⅝	⅜
Full	18	A1	72	4	29	⅞
		A2	72	4	29	⅞
		B1	72	4	15½	½
		B2	144	8	31	⅞
		B3	72	4	15½	½
Queen	25	A1	100	5	36¼	1⅛
		A2	100	5	36¼	1⅛
		B1	100	5	19⅜	⅝
		B2	200	10	38¾	1⅛
		B3	100	5	19⅜	⅝
King	41	A1	164	9	65¼	1⅞
		A2	164	9	65¼	1⅞
		B1	164	9	34⅞	1
		B2	328	17	65⅞	1⅞
		B3	164	9	34⅞	1

Sister's Choice

Piece	1st Cut Strip Width	2nd Cut Dimensions	No. of Pieces from 1 Strip	3rd Cut
A	3"	Template A*	7	
B	3⅜"	3⅜" x 3⅜"	12	24 ◻
C1	3"	3" x 3"	14	
C2	3"	3" x 3"	14	
D	2½"	3" x 2½"	14	
E	2½"	2½" x 2½"	16	

*Page 38

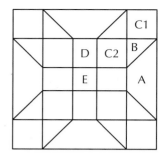

Sister's Choice

Quilt Size	No. of Blocks	Piece	No. of Pieces	No. of Strips to Cut	Yardage Required In Inches	In Yards
Wall	5	A	20	3	9	¼
		B	40	2	6¾	¼
		C1	20	2	6	¼
		C2	20	2	6	¼
		D	20	2	5	¼
		E	5	1	2½	⅛
Crib	6	A	24	4	12	⅓
		B	48	2	6¾	¼
		C1	24	2	6	¼
		C2	24	2	6	¼
		D	24	2	5	¼
		E	6	1	2½	⅛
Twin	14	A	56	8	24	⅔
		B	112	5	16⅞	½
		C1	56	4	12	⅓
		C2	56	4	12	⅓
		D	56	4	10	⅜
		E	14	1	2½	⅛
Full	18	A	72	11	33	1
		B	144	6	20¼	⅝
		C1	72	6	18	½
		C2	72	6	18	½
		D	72	6	15	½
		E	18	2	5	¼
Queen	25	A	100	15	45	1¼
		B	200	9	30⅜	⅞
		C1	100	8	20	⅝
		C2	100	8	20	⅝
		D	100	8	20	⅝
		E	25	2	5	¼
King	41	A	164	24	72	2
		B	328	14	47¼	1⅜
		C1	164	12	36	1
		C2	164	12	36	1
		D	164	12	30	⅞
		E	41	3	7½	¼

Pine Burr

Piece	1st Cut Strip Width	2nd Cut Dimensions	No. of Pieces from 1 Strip	3rd Cut
A	4"	4" x 4"	10	
B	3⅜"	3⅜" x 3⅜"	12	24 ◺
C	4⅜"	4⅜" x 4⅜"	9	18 ◺
D1	2⅞"	2⅞" x 2⅞"	14	28 ◺
D2	2⅞"	2⅞" x 2⅞"	14	28 ◺
E	3"	2½" x 3"	16	

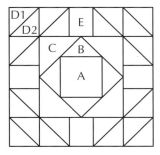

Pine Burr

Quilt Size	No. of Blocks	Piece	No. of Pieces	No. of Strips to Cut	Yardage Required In Inches	In Yards
Wall	5	A	5	1	4	⅛
		B	20	1	3⅜	⅛
		C	20	2	8¾	¼
		D1	60	3	8⅝	¼
		D2	60	3	8⅝	¼
		E	20	2	6	¼
Crib	6	A	6	1	4	⅛
		B	24	1	3⅜	⅛
		C	24	2	8¾	¼
		D1	72	3	8⅝	¼
		D2	72	3	8⅝	¼
		E	24	2	6	¼
Twin	14	A	14	2	8	¼
		B	56	3	10⅛	⅓
		C	56	4	17½	½
		D1	168	6	17¼	½
		D2	168	6	17¼	½
		E	56	4	12	⅓
Full	18	A	18	2	8	¼
		B	72	4	13½	½
		C	72	4	17½	½
		D1	216	8	23	¾
		D2	216	8	23	¾
		E	72	5	15	½
Queen	25	A	25	3	12	⅓
		B	100	5	16⅞	½
		C	100	6	26¼	¾
		D1	300	11	31⅝	1
		D2	300	11	31⅝	1
		E	100	7	21	⅝
King	41	A	41	5	12	⅓
		B	164	7	23⅝	¾
		C	164	10	43¾	1¼
		D1	492	18	51¾	1½
		D2	492	18	51¾	1½
		E	164	11	33	1

Ohio Star

Piece	1st Cut Strip Width	Additional Cuts 2nd Cut Dimensions	No. of Pieces from 1 Strip	3rd Cut
A	4½"	4½" x 4½"	9	
B1	5¼"	5¼" x 5¼"	8	32 ⊠
B2	5¼"	5¼" x 5¼"	8	32 ⊠
B3	5¼"	5¼" x 5¼"	8	32 ⊠
C*	4½"	4½" x 4½"	9	
D	3⅜"	3⅜" 3⅜"	12	24 ◺

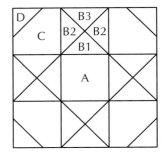

Ohio Star

*Use Cut-off Template A on page 68 to remove one corner of each 4½" square for C.

Quilt Size	No. of Blocks	Piece	No. of Pieces	No. of Strips to Cut	Yardage Required In Inches	In Yards
Wall	5	A	5	1	4½	⅛
		B1	20	1	5¼	⅛
		B2	40	2	10½	⅓
		B3	20	1	5¼	⅛
		C	20	3	13½	½
		D	20	1	3⅜	⅛
Wall	6	A	6	1	4½	⅛
		B1	24	1	5¼	⅛
		B2	48	2	10½	⅓
		B3	24	1	5¼	⅛
		C	24	3	13½	½
		D	24	1	3⅜	⅛
Twin	14	A	14	2	9	¼
		B1	56	2	10½	⅓
		B2	112	4	21	⅝
		B3	56	2	10½	⅓
		C	56	7	31½	1
		D	56	3	10¼	⅓
Full	18	A	18	2	9	¼
		B1	72	3	15¾	½
		B2	144	5	26¼	¾
		B3	72	3	15¾	½
		C	72	8	36	1
		D	72	3	10¼	⅓
Queen	25	A	25	3	13½	⅜
		B1	100	4	21	⅝
		B2	200	7	36¾	1⅛
		B3	100	4	21	⅝
		C	100	12	54	1½
		D	100	5	16⅞	½
King	41	A	41	5	22½	⅝
		B1	164	6	31½	⅞
		B2	328	11	57¾	1⅝
		B3	164	6	31½	⅞
		C	164	19	85½	2⅜
		D	164	7	23⅝	¾

Shoofly

Piece	1st Cut Strip Width	Additional Cuts 2nd Cut Dimensions	No. of Pieces from 1 Strip	3rd Cut
A	4½"	4½" x 4½"	9	
B	4½"	4½" x 4½"	9	
C1	4⅞"	4⅞" x 4⅞"	8	16 ◪
C2	4⅞"	4⅞" x 4⅞"	8	16 ◪

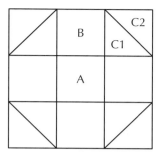

Shoofly

Quilt Size	No. of Blocks	Piece	No. of Pieces	No. of Strips to Cut	Yardage Required In Inches	In Yards
Wall	5	A	5	1	4½	⅛
		B	20	3	13½	⅜
		C1	20	2	9¾	⅓
		C2	20	2	9¾	⅓
Crib	6	A	6	1	4½	⅛
		B	24	3	13½	⅜
		C1	24	2	9¾	⅓
		C2	24	2	9¾	⅓
Twin	14	A	14	2	9	¼
		B	56	7	31½	⅞
		C1	56	4	19½	⅝
		C2	56	4	19½	⅝
Full	18	A	18	2	9	¼
		B	72	8	36	1
		C1	72	5	24⅜	¾
		C2	72	5	24⅜	¾
Queen	25	A	25	3	13½	⅜
		B	100	12	54	1½
		C1	100	7	34⅛	1
		C2	100	7	34⅛	1
King	41	A	41	5	22½	⅝
		B	164	19	85½	2⅜
		C1	164	11	53⅝	1½
		C2	164	11	53⅝	1½

Churn Dash

Piece	1st Cut Strip Width	2nd Cut Dimensions	No. of Pieces from 1 Strip	3rd Cut
A	4½"	4½" x 4½"	9	
B1	2½"	2½" x 4½"	9	
B2	2½"	2½" x 4½"	9	
C1	4⅞"	4⅞" x 4⅞"	8	16 ◺
C2	4⅞"	4⅞" x 4⅞"	8	16 ◺

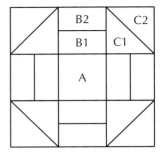

Churn Dash

Quilt Size	No. of Blocks	Piece	No. of Pieces	No. of Strips to Cut	Yardage Required In Inches	In Yards
Wall	5	A	5	1	4½	⅛
		B1	20	3	7½	¼
		B2	20	3	7½	¼
		C1	20	2	9¾	⅓
		C2	20	2	9¾	⅓
Crib	6	A	6	1	4½	⅛
		B1	24	3	7½	¼
		B2	24	3	7½	¼
		C1	24	2	9¾	⅓
		C2	24	2	9¾	⅓
Twin	14	A	14	2	9	¼
		B1	56	7	17½	½
		B2	56	7	17½	½
		C1	56	4	19½	⅝
		C2	56	4	19½	⅝
Full	18	A	18	2	9	¼
		B1	72	8	20	⅝
		B2	72	8	20	⅝
		C1	72	5	24⅜	¾
		C2	72	5	24⅜	¾
Queen	25	A	25	3	13½	⅜
		B1	100	12	30	⅞
		B2	100	12	30	⅞
		C1	100	7	34⅛	1
		C2	100	7	34⅛	1
King	41	A	41	5	22½	⅝
		B1	164	19	47½	1⅜
		B2	164	19	47½	1⅜
		C1	164	11	53⅝	1½
		C2	164	11	53⅝	1½

Broken Wheel

Piece	1st Cut Strip Width	Additional Cuts 2nd Cut Dimensions	No. of Pieces from 1 Strip	3rd Cut
A	4½"	4½" x 4½"	9	
B1	2½"	2½" x 4½"	9	
B2	2½"	2½" x 4½"	9	
C	2⅞"	2⅞" x 2⅞"	14	28 ◰
D	3⅜"	3⅜" x 3⅜"	12	

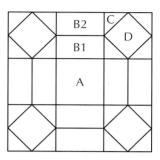

Broken Wheel

Quilt Size	No. of Blocks	Piece	No. of Pieces	No. of Strips to Cut	Yardage Required In Inches	In Yards
Wall	5	A	5	1	4½	⅛
		B1	20	3	7½	¼
		B2	20	3	7½	¼
		C	80	3	8⅝	¼
		D	20	2	6¾	¼
Crib	6	A	6	1	4½	⅛
		B1	24	3	7½	¼
		B2	24	3	7½	¼
		C	96	4	8⅝	¼
		D	24	2	6¾	¼
Twin	14	A	14	2	9	¼
		B1	56	7	17½	½
		B2	56	7	17½	½
		C	224	8	23	¾
		D	56	5	16⅞	½
Full	18	A	18	2	9	¼
		B1	72	8	20	⅝
		B2	72	8	20	⅝
		C	288	11	31⅝	1
		D	72	6	20¼	⅝
Queen	25	A	25	3	13½	⅜
		B1	100	12	30	⅞
		B2	100	12	30	⅞
		C	400	15	43⅛	1¼
		D	100	9	30⅜	⅞
King	41	A	41	5	22½	⅝
		B1	164	19	47½	1⅜
		B2	164	19	47½	1⅜
		C	656	24	69	2
		D	164	14	47¼	1⅜

About the Author

Deborah J. Moffett-Hall's quilt-design career began in 1989 when one of her patterns appeared in *Quilt Magazine*. She is currently Special Projects Editor for *Quilt, Country Quilts,* and *Old Fashioned Patchwork*, and a contributing editor for other magazines. More than ninety of Deborah's designs have been featured in major magazines. Three of Deborah's designs can be seen in *Quilted for Christmas* and one in *Quilted for Christmas, Book II* (That Patchwork Place). This is her first solo book.

In between sewing the projects for *Traditional Blocks Meet Appliqué*, Deborah and her family sold their home and moved to a larger house in the same neighborhood. Deborah now has her own studio, and the family is happy to have the sewing machine off the dining room table. Deborah also has room for her industrial quilting machine and offers machine-quilting services to other quilters.

Deborah lives in Hatfield, Pennsylvania, with her husband, Scott, and daughter, Michelle. Deborah considers herself lucky to have such a supportive family. Scott can name most traditional quilt patterns at a glance, and Michelle is designing quilt blocks on their home computer.

Notes:

That Patchwork Place Publications and Products